Blaming No One

Blaming No One

Blog postings on arts, letters, policy

Dan Whitman

VELLUM   NAP   NEW ACADEMIA
PUBLISHING

Washington, DC

Library of Congress Control Number: 2012942292
ISBN 978-0-9855698-6-0 paperback (alk. paper)

VELLUM   An imprint of New Academia Publishing

NEW ACADEMIA
PUBLISHING

New Academia Publishing
PO Box 27420, Washington, DC 20038-7420
info@newacademia.com - www.newacademia.com

Contents

Introduction: What If?   ix
Reader's Manual   xii

Not the Gbagbo I Knew   1
With a Thousand Pictures, Nothing is Still Nothing   4
Of Apes and Arms: When Brains Prevail   7
The Bark is Worse   10
Is There a Fool in the House?   12
My Moment with P.J.   15
Isidorus Rex (1907-1989)   19
Amazing Grace and… a Touch of Vodou   23
Pax Vobiscum Alex   27
Mission Possible in Munich   31
Why is This Man Smiling?   35
If Music Be the Food   38
Coping with Opus   41
Totentanz at Orly   44
PD on the House   49
Many Would Rescue, Few Would Help   53
Herodotus of Arlington, Virginia   56
Looking into the Sun   59
Ten Out, Ninety to Go   62

vi

The Case for Aid 64

The Importance 67

When Slava Met Yo-Yo 70

At Peace with Nukes? 73

Looking Back and Fourth 76

Death Warmed Over in Yaoundé 79

A Summer Read for Our Time 82

Boom to Bust to Deductible: Hegel Knows Best 86

Smith-Mundt, R.I.P. 89

Guinea on My Mind 92

Konaté's Speech 96

Peek-a-Boo 100

In Boca di Lobo 104

Getting to YES 107

Let Them Show Us 110

Trapezoids 113

Again to the Breach 116

Another Chance for DRC 120

While They Slept 122

Sandy and Henri 126

Jacques Among the Living 128

At It Again 132

Sarith's Story 135

My Southeast Asia 138

Blaming No One 141

Bad Boy Gbagbo 144

In a Name 146

An Ambassador Speaks 150

All Power to the 164th 154

Christmas in Lunel 156

Zelig at INF 160

"In Some Village, an Idiot Goes Missing…"   164

Open Season on War Crimes   167

Stalin Without the Bullets   171

Lavrov Crunched   174

Shovels to Anguissa   177

Chekhov's Garden   181

An Artist's Finest Moment   184

Stolen Sandwiches   188

The Devil's Due   190

UNESCO's Bad   194

The Window That Went Around the World   198

Declinism in Decline   201

Lunch with Joe   205

Our Next Bubble   210

This Week in Africa, Good News and Bad   213

Cosmogony in a Coffee Tin   217

Inuits, Whales, Bach   221

Malamud and Me   224

The Sinologist in Each of Us   227

At the Feet of the Master   230

Sony Lab'ou Tansi (1947-1995)   233

Lowering the Volume   237

"Please Go Away"   241

Introduction

What If?

Imagine Michel de Montaigne under an 800-word limit. I don't mean to compare my little pieces or myself to the one who started us on sharing personal reflections. Yet the thought keeps coming back. Montaigne would have (a) chafed against a limit so artificial, (b) tossed it aside disdainfully, or (c) taken to it comfortably. All we know for sure is that, in his case, rage or indignation would not have been factors.

I can't say that Montaigne "inspired" these efforts, but he did establish the Self as a subject worthy of others' attention. The time and space we inhabit is not comparable to his: ambient warfare and neighborhood atrocities his only distraction, he had a castle tower and tons of time. We of the twenty-first century might have fixed his gallstones for him, but could never have made conditions propitious for economic indifference or the seclusion we all say we crave, but never make for ourselves.

Personally I like the 800-word form. It came from the editor who carried my first blog – the one about Laurent Gbagbo which follows. I was neither pro nor con, just wanted to surface the idea. Conformity to the form was the price of doing so. As I wrote it on April 5, 2011, I thought, "Whoa, this actually suits me." No straightjacket, no Procrustean beds. Something about it was pleasing, and led me to write more. I never sought or received money for any blogs, nor frankly even wide readership. Having them "out there" (read: preserved and accessible) was the main motivation. This may sound coy, but it's true.

A blog is not an *"essai,"* it's just a blog. As one friend put it to me, it's an hors d'oeuvre. He didn't mean to trivialize my content, nor did I take it that way. An hors d'oeuvre whets the appetite. Even at their most contemplative and human moments, people "whet" appetites (that is, create them), so as later to sate them. Satiation is an elusive goal, so we often are left with wanting, more than having, and it seems we almost like it that way. Yes, it's a perversion, but every vice has its corresponding virtue, and humans deal with both, all the time. The corresponding virtue here is movement and dynamism. We are not meant to be fixed in time and space. We have plane tickets, Skype, tele-this and tele-that which Montaigne never needed or lacked. See Emily Dickinson on this subject.

The blog form has something to do with friendship, which is a very high value to me, higher anyway than freedom or the type of morality that can be checked by bar code. Friendship's dialogues are too seldom captured, its cherishable moments too easily dispelled. "Too seldom" and "too easily" only in the sense of wanting to get my druthers, and I don't always get those. So I whet, then I see about satiation.

Interaction takes place in time and space, and works best when interlocutors can converse in a room. The things you do together can be chronicled or recorded, but what you say will define, establish, and perpetuate the friendship. It defies permanence, though, and is not usually available to others. I'm not advocating exhibitionism.

Setting these conversational moments in amber (the blog) does not make up a noticeable human advancement, but it does scratch an itch.

Blogs to me have to do with how people spend time together, including a moment together with a reader I may never know. The 800-word limit somehow assures that the blog gets written and, more importantly, thought. The conversations themselves are records of what we think, and "to think" – well, enough centuries and energies have gone into figuring out the nature of that. As with our biologies, the specialists may have reason to understand them, the rest of us just put them to use when we're lucky and things work.

Make what you will of these reflections. Some are topical, others non-temporal observations. I hope they may lighten moments on a plane or in a waiting room. Receive them with my cordial thanks. If I say "I don't need you to read these," I am being permissive, not dismissive. I don't exaggerate the importance of "my world" but I welcome you to enter it.

For me, a blog is a thought. It is more pleasing to have a thought than to postpone it. Classical theater had enormous suspense and appeal, more for what it could not and did not say, than what it said. Nowadays we say nearly anything, but the 800-word limit removes the helium and gets us on a single topic for the time span of a thought. Limits thereby ease and comfort us. And there go my 799 words, so I guess I'll stop.

Reader's Manual

The blog postings in this volume are sequential and chronological, but I allow and urge you to read them in no particular order. Just note the date of each, for indications of my prescience in cases of political commentary.

About the 800 word limit. A number of these pieces creep around the arbitrary limit, like crabgrass. What is one to do, but favor tolerance for deviations?

I acknowledge and thank Mark Tapscott of the *Examiner* for his encouragement and publication of the first piece, on Laurent Gbagbo. Likewise Norbert Tchana Ngante in Douala, Cameroon, for the second on *Africa-Info.org*. All others come with my gratitude to American University's Punditwire, a blog site for former speech writers. I had no idea I might qualify for such an august group, until Bob Lehrman said to me, "Well, you used to write speeches for ambassadors overseas, didn't you?"

And indeed I did. Twenty-five years lashed to the mast of United States public diplomacy postings in Copenhagen, Madrid, Pretoria, Port-au-Prince, Yaoundé, Conakry, Accra. Such richness of experience, so one-sided, the benefits! I marvel over those moments of personal discovery (1985-2009) and camaraderie with some remarkable colleagues.

The postings in this book, however, stray from the confines of my various jobs, and certainly from PPP – pure political punditry.

"Punditwire" of course is a term coined tongue in cheek, as no one admits to the title of "pundit" but in ironical self deprecation.

Mary Robbins and Aaron Rockett have been most marvelous in their loving care of this invigorating site, and long may it live. Kari Jaksa, Sara Wotman, and Margery Thompson were unerring friends in spiffing up these texts. Two hundred lunches for Sara. She knows why. Kari was muse, *rédactrice extraordinaire*, manager. Banalities and errors of course are only mine. Typos belong to the Constellations.

I recommend this book for air travelers who may have a nap or a meal in the near future. These comments appear to be stand-alone reflections, none dependent on its preceding or following post. Heck, read a few, leave the book in the seat back pocket for others, and then buy another when you find you wanted more after all.

The postings here reproduced were all "published" in a one-year period, from spring 2011 to spring 2012. I guess they constitute views, notions, reactions, and autobiographical fragments. Of Francis Bacon's options I see them as readings to be tasted, chewed, not necessarily "swallowed," even if swallowed sounds better.

My wish is for some moments of combined and shared thought, certainly not notoriety or profit. For those, I will turn to other irresponsible pursuits.

Dan Whitman

May, 2012

Not the Gbagbo I Knew

April 6, 2011

Reprinted from the *Examiner*

By the time you read this, Cote d'Ivoire's president and strong-arm dictator Laurent Gbagbo will be out or in, alive, dead, or in flight. He's not about to return as the friend I knew in 1980 when he traveled to the U.S.

At that time, Laurent wasn't even of the rank of *enfant terrible*, though he strived to be. With others, I served as his interpreter, chauffeur, drinking partner, and foxhole comrade. Those who knew him found him funny. He had us in stitches.

Gbagbo, an historian, traveled to seven states in five weeks that year with Operation Crossroads Africa. Crossroaders were familial, adventurous, willing to live and travel in basic accommodations, open to mutual discovery.

Laurent was selected from a competitive pool, and financed, by the U.S. Embassy in Abidjan, as a "Young African Leader." The irony here is striking, but does not impugn the fine work of U.S. government educational and cultural exchange over six decades.

Laurent was one of Africa's benchwarmers, hoping for a brighter time when their countries would correct their courses and accountability would prevail. The term "kleptocracy" came up in the 1970s, and with it, the hurtful stereotypes of African rulers more out for themselves than for the well-being of their countrymen.

I remember Laurent's railings against his country's president at that time, the long ruling Felix Houphouet-Boigny. Laurent saw Houphouet as a ruthless dictator, and knew he could do better.

He had unlikely schemes to replace him one day, and amazingly he did, after two unsuccessful attempts. I wasn't even sure if he would make it through in one piece, judging from his own horror stories about his country's regime at the time. He was a utopian. Utopians don't usually take over countries.

What happened, then? How do humans become the very oppressors they spend their energies and equities to remove? Shakespeare and Verdi blamed it on the wife behind the throne. Of this I know nothing.

And yet, have better explanations come along? Inspired leaders go rancid too often not to beggar explanation. We ignore this quirk at our peril, a science should be cobbled together ASAP to see why these things happen.

The Laurent I knew wouldn't spill his countrymen's blood even if the UN, U.S., EU, and AU had all been mistaken in declaring Alassane Ouattara the winner of the 2010 elections. My Laurent was inclined to compassion over others' misfortunes. A sadist he was not.

Lessons learned? People change. A lot. So far, the variables and causes have eluded social scientists, psychologists, political strategists. A little humility here: We need to figure this out, and fast. I don't follow: how could a fun-loving person willingly harm his country for an unattainable degree of self aggrandizement? The train has no brakes, we'd better retrofit them wherever we can.

Another Shakespeare character would have picked up the skull of the demised, and said, "Alas, poor Laurent! I knew him, Horatio." But that was at a kinder time, when a single person could disappear safely to obscurity.

With a Thousand Pictures, Nothing is Still Nothing

April 18, 2011

Reprinted from *Africa-Info.org*

December 30, 1941, Armenian-born photographer Yousuf Karsh got a photo session with Winston Churchill, after the latter's speech to Canadian Parliament during Britain's darkest days of World War II. Unable to get the look of defiance he thought was needed for the occasion, Karsh ripped the cigar from Churchill's hand. The iconic photo resulted, with Churchill's famous scowl.

April 11, 2011, photographers recorded the apprehension of Cote d'Ivoire's now ex- president, Laurent Gbagbo. Take any news service you want, but the Reuters version shows the bewilderment of a wronged three-year-old boy with his red fire engine taken away. In this case it was a nation state of 21 million inhabitants, the world's largest cocoa producer, with a per capita GDP of $1800. Cote d'Ivoire, once the economic engine of francophone West Africa, emerged, barely, from five months of one giant toothache as its president refused to accept the outcome of the November, 2010 elections. Order restored, sort of. The Great Birnham Woods did to Dunsinane march, and the community was restored to relative sanity. Election winner Alassane Ouattara showed magnanimity in assuring Gbagbo's physical well-being while assuring a trial to determine the latter's possible human rights violations.

Classical theater shows us that the boy with the fire engine is the more interesting character than the one who restores the community. The former is usually a tenor in the opera version, the latter a bass-baritone. In Calderón de la Barca's seventeenth-century classic, a cranky Pedro Crespo gets to be mayor of Zalamea and behaves badly, as does his mistress Chispa. The fuss is brought into line by the king's soldiers. In the Soviet version, the people—not the central government authority—take things into their own hands.

Bullies have whipped us around since the invention of speech, and probably even before. No one has yet figured out how to confine them, other than laboriously beating them at their own game – usually with unacceptable numbers of casualties. It gets to be labor intensive to do so.

Think of the little gangster Abimael *Guzman* arrested in Peru in 1992 and put on trial as the magus behind the Sendero Luminoso in Peru. Or the pudgy Buddha, Aum Shinrikyo, who staged murderous sarin chemical attacks in the Tokyo subway in 1995. Unmasked, they usually turn out to be punks.

With Divine Right out of style and monarchies no longer keeping temporal structures on an even keel, we seem to have only fiction and theater to address the monstrous wrongs done to us. Gorgeous opera can result, but this is the Real Thing. The question arises, why maintain vertical, hierarchical structures at all, if this is the best we can do?

I am not talking anarchy here, or world government. Sovereignty is the model we have before us, until something better comes along.

Once the fools, the bullies, are unmasked, they are shown to be mollusks without their protective shells, as in the unforgettable photos of Laurent Gbagbo that hit the wires April 12, the day after his arrest. The vulnerability of the invertebrates at the hour of their reckoning does not give us blood lust, but more sadness at their bewilderment, and at our own inability to defend ourselves against them.

The good news for the Christian Laurent Gbagbo (Alassane Ouattara is Muslim) is that he enjoys continued support from Senator James M. Inhofe, (R-OK). Quoted by the *Foreign Policy* blog April 14, he said, "It is more of a Jesus thing, but I have spent a lot of time in Africa."

My understanding is that Jesus meant for authority to be taken away from abusers and given to the Meek. High time for this to happen. No more Gbagbos please, and in the meantime let's at least keep them distracted with the fire engines they crave.

A university in Boston offered Gbagbo a professorship some weeks ago, as incentive to give up power in Cote d'Ivoire. Nice gesture. But imagine sharing an office space with him. Would you leave your own red fire engine overnight in the office?

Of Apes and Arms: When Brains Prevail

April 27, 2011

It started seven years ago with one man's empathy for chimps –
those little guys with DNA 98 percent like our own. (When I broke
my thumb once, the doctor said, "Now you are one percent closer
to being a chimp," but that was another story.)

Ofir Drori, Israeli eccentric and transplant, fell in love with Cameroon and all things African, and took a do-gooder approach of saving chimps, even as the humans needed a ton of saving as well.
The result was LAGA—the Last Great Ape Organization—based
in Yaoundé.

Drawing fully on the only interdiction tool he had—chutzpah—
Ofir engaged brain and proceeded. He improvised his own plea
bargains, confronting big contraband gangsters with partial details
of their misdeeds, and getting them to rat on one another. How he
got past the doors of the *padrinos*, or why he has been left unmo-
lested to this day, kneecaps intact, is a secret best known by him.
In countries with the best justice money can buy—Cameroon,

Chad, Central African Republic, Congo, Gabon—Ofir got an 83 percent incarceration rate from those he went after. Clang-clang, case closed. It's a miracle.

Wait, though – just picking at the scabs of ape abuse, and by the way, illegal ivory harvesting, LAGA found huge additional sores underneath: the same networks that shipped tons of contraband ivory to unscrupulous buyers in Taiwan often slipped arms, narcotics, and cash into the containers for delivery. NGO private wildlife law enforcement began doing for governments what governments were not positioned to do themselves. It turns out that needlessly torturing apes is unsettlingly akin to other forms of personal gain which can do in the humans as well. Who would have thought?
The UN, World Wildlife Fund, and U.S. Fisheries and Wildlife Service all took notice. A lone individual cracked a code, and by the way, got awards from the Secretary General of the UN Convention on Trade in Endangered Species (CITES).

With Ofir's brainy methodology even child trafficking gets on the agenda, with Catholic Relief Services now picking up on his model. Transparency International also followed his approach, and set up an anti-corruption hotline to flush out corrupt judges and officials who are more part of the problem than the solution.

In seven years, LAGA has appeared in 366 media pieces and gotten 59,000 views on YouTube. With no government authority (but with cooperation from the latter), LAGA has conducted 244 investigations, and in one case nabbed 21 major dealers in five days. Prosecution? LAGA gives full documentation in 85 percent of the cases, and gets 83 per cent in jail.

Abducting an African grey parrot, or a sea turtle, leads in a more or less direct line to contraband and the corruption that robs African people of 25-50 percent of their wealth per year. You don't have to love chimps, but it helps. Corrupt regimes even turn state's evidence, caught up in the exhilaration of the process. Most people don't really prefer to be enemies of humanity, as long as it's rewarding and fun to join the Other Side.

LAGA puts out a press release every day – that would make over 2,000 to date. They have maintained a stable rate of one arrest per week for the past six years, and have put over 350 dealers behind bars. LAGA has documented that in over 80 percent of its cases, bribing attempts would have averted justice if LAGA had not intervened.

Ofir is still basically a one-man operation, and yes, he needs money in order to keep going. Have a look at his website www.laga-enforcement.org.

The Bark is Worse

April 28, 2011

I swear I did not pass this picture through Photoshop or any other type of *trompe-l'oeil* process.

Do dogs read English? If they did, would they follow the dictates of messages directed to them? Papua New Guinea has 0.01 percent of the world's population, but 25 percent of the world's languages. Could it be that American dogs are conversant in one or more of the latter?

My point here is that someone argued a case and came to a resolution. The bark lobbyists met the anti-barks, and a town hall process came up with a consensus, allowing all parties some measure of comfort.

I won't say, "We are a litigious nation." That is a commonplace. But it seems we reserve our rage and passions for trivia. Could this be a dark scheme to distract us from the real threats to our species, like climate change, children trafficked, Stinger missiles in the hands of drugged prepubescent boys, and intractable ethnic conflict?

I don't begrudge people's need to argue and find common solutions. I'm even glad that the town hall meeting has replaced, mostly, the use of the shotgun as a way of settling disputes. Neighbors within view of the sign in the photograph, however, have actually said to dog owners, "The value of my property is going down!" As well it might. Enmities remain and bitter feelings infiltrate the neighborhood. Man's Best Friend poops recklessly in the space provided to do so. People reach new paradigms in finding things to differ over.

Humans are split into dualities: male-female, nomadic-sedentary, anima-animus... The one we deal with here, however, is...how to say...those who would live and let live, versus those who would tell us (and dogs) how and when to do their business, and at what decibel level. Call them orthodox versus laissez-faire, I guess.
For me, the orthodox are the enemy, but I would never say so to one of them, as I know I'd go straight to the wheel for breaking, or to the stake. I'm not saying they break and burn just for pleasure – surely they do so as a last resort after exhausting other means of convincing us to be like them.

But don't they realize that a thousand girls a minute are being impressed into slavery world-wide, and that we will all die?

I would say they are stupid, but what do I know? I only know one to see one, and always try to step aside when they come after us laissez-faire people with a cleaver.

Is There a Fool in the House?

April 28, 2011

April 7 of this year the Aspen Institute pulled together a remark-able feat, assembling three former Secretaries of State—Baker, Al-bright, and Powell—to reflect in the National Cathedral about the meeting point of personal conviction and national interest. Aspen's president, Walter Isaacson, maybe the only person who could mea-sure up to moderating such a thing, kept the dialogue at a brisk pace, admirably drawing out each former SecState in roughly equal amounts.

Imagine, personal values on the same playbill as national interest. And in a cathedral.

On one point Isaacson, invoking the absent Donald Rumsfeld, bait-ed Powell: "Rumsfeld says you are wrong on this." *Toro, toro!*
It seemed scripted: after less than a five-second delay, Powell said of the former SecDef, "Rumsfeld's memoirs are something between deceptive and illusory." Those were his exact words. Lots of people wrote them down.

Astonishment filled the expansive hall, and 2,000 listeners stirred, exclaimed, howled, laughed. A few started to applaud, but then stopped in mid-clap. This was, after all, the venue where George W. Bush declared war on September 14, 2001. Imams weren't supposed to use mosques for this purpose, but cathedrals must be different.

On the April 7 incident, I know you might not believe this happened, since no news source reported it. But I assure you it did, and on the record. Powell finally got to say in public what had been on his mind for eight years. Maybe it was even pre-arranged with moderator Isaacson, who looked pretty pleased to have set off a sulfurous chain reaction.

Now skip to April 22, when the Associated Press got hold of an advance copy of UN Chief Nuclear Inspector Mohamed El Baradei's new book, *The Age of Deception*. Nobel Peace Prize winner El Baradei picks out the period 2002-2003 as one of the "shame of a needless war." During this period, of course, all the world knew the tensions between Rumsfeld and Powell, and their rivalry. Notwithstanding, the team pulled together and claimed or feigned threat of WMD from Iraq in February of 2003, and into the UN Security Council session of March 7, 2003, leading to UNSC Resolution 1441 on March 17. After false British intelligence had been cited ten weeks earlier in the January 28, 2003, State of the Union address, SecState Condoleeza Rice had aptly noted, "[Sheesh,] it was only thirteen words." She kept the refrain going into March.

(One imagines other thirteen-word statements of levity, like, "I will tear your tongue from your head and roast your testicles good.") Mohamed El Baradei knows from WMD, and now in 2011 calls for a criminal investigation of the whole team. You're killing me, Mohamed, I'm pulling a stomach muscle from laughing.

In Seville, Spain, my friend was accosted by a shoeshine man wanting to polish her canvas running shoes. She said in her perfect Spanish, "Look. Someone here is an idiot. Either you or me." In defense of the shoeshine man, it could have been possible that my friend might have been the idiot. In such a case, anything goes. As it does with our voters – note the conciliatory manner in which I say that, where reds and blues can each find truth in the same statement.

Back to Powell v. Rumsfeld, with the others comfortably not present: what if we were to accept the evidence we now have, that the whole team lied? Would anyone mind, and would the team unravel as the one pointed a finger at the other to cop a plea?

And when a man is killed in war, is he less dead if the "Laws of War" were scrupulously adhered to in the killing?

Stop, please! My laughter is half way to rictus, I could get an embolism if you keep on.

My Moment with P.J.

May 1, 2011

I always liked P.J. Crowley. You won't find many people saying so in public these days, especially after March 12 when he became radioactive. That was when he said the conditions of detention of Private Bradley Manning, a Wikileaks source, were "ridiculous and counterproductive and stupid." With some hullabaloo, Crowley was bounced the next day as spokesman for the U.S. Department of State. Asked if he had thought about repenting, on March 27 he said, "I don't regret saying what I said…I spoke my mind and I haven't changed my view."

Look him up on the Internet these days. You'll see a whole lot about the wax melting from his wings of Icarus that day in March, but almost nothing about who he is and what he did to make the State Department more credible.

First of all, how can one dislike a person who publishes his name in a form that means "nightwear." Crowley does have a first name from birth, which is "Philip." I haven't seen the long form birth certificate (July 28, 1951), but "Philip" seems like an OK name to me, even dignified. Maybe too much so for P.J., who I guess picked it up somewhere in school in Brockton, Massachusetts, and allowed it to stick into adulthood.

Crowley's father spent two years as a POW in an East German prison camp. P.J. himself served 26 years in the U.S. Air Force, and got to work with Javier Solana, Secretary General of NATO, from April to June, 1999. He was Assistant Secretary of State for Public Affairs from May 26, 2009, to March 13, 2011.

Though I never drafted texts for Crowley, I was briefly part of his world, and I always felt he served the Department well.

I had a single moment with him in June, 2009. He gathered any of us who could make it over to the Public Affairs office on a couple hours notice, to meet him after he replaced Sean McCormack as spokesman. About forty of us got to the meeting. We mostly knew one another, as the PA world is finite.

Crowley was affable, engaging, and open-minded. American officials talk a lot about "listening" and generally do very little of it in fact. Crowley was in genuine listening mode that day. I mean, really.

He asked for feedback, comments, advice. As often happens in any organization at such times, discomfort happened, and no one knew what to say or do. He asked twice, three times, but met the trepidation of bureaucrats fearing a trap set by the new boss we didn't know yet.

I applied my "Rule of Three," and raised my hand only the after the third time he asked and no one else had a thing to say. I knew I'd be retiring from DoS soon enough.

"Mr. Crowley, I hope the State Department can say things more clearly now with you here, say things it really means. If we did, people might start listening to us." I am paraphrasing, I don't remember the exact words.

A high ranking colleague countered me: "But journalists do listen to us. They pay a lot of attention to the things we say."

In for a dime, in for a dollar. I answered, "Right. And the reason they parse our words is that we say so little, and they are trying to pick up any nuggets of actual content that might slip through the clearance process."

People in the room laughed a little, and so did Crowley. We're talking about a considerable apparatus which issued basically a one-size-fits-all statement most days for most topics: "We view the situation with concern, and are monitoring it closely. We call on all parties for restraint, and look forward to a speedy resolution." Pablum, I think.

Crowley took the point in his gracious way. I never saw him again. I wish I could say, "…And the tone of State Department statements became clearer and more substantive following my comment," but that would be self serving. I can't prove it, but I think the voice of the State Department did become more clear during that period. Crowley should get lots of credit for this, I accept none. The Department actually said things and people did start to listen. It's always an imperfect process, one step forward, three steps back, as during SecState Clinton's first trip to Beijing, where she gave the Chinese government a pass on human rights. But this was a work in progress, and she got it right the second time, and should be noted for doing so.

I like my State Department colleagues a lot. They are smart, they try hard, and they care.

Of course there are those few who spoil it for the rest of us, the Mad Hatter types who say things like "Lack of political will!" – a phrase that has never meant anything at all to me. ("Squark! Squark! Lack of political will! Squark!") I think people who cling to these empty phrases may be victims of Tourette Syndrome.

P.J. Crowley didn't have Tourette's. He thought, then spoke, and he did so in the spirit of the Department at its best. One day we will see how he added to DoS's greatest asset: credibility.

Crowley lived the dream of every bureaucrat. When he saw it was time to leave, he went entirely rogue, just once. Setting the record straight after his career's destruction, he said "The United States, as an exceptional country in the world, has to be seen as practicing what we preach."

I think it's also called "going out with a bang." Exiting stage left, he said, "I'm not a larger-than-life person. I'm short, bald, and old."

Tall enough to reach the ground, as Abe Lincoln would have said. And one day I hope to see P.J. again, and tell him so in person.

Isidorus Rex (1907-1989)

May 7, 2011

Isidor Feinstein Stone was pretty much whatever you wanted to think about him: champion of truth, bad boy, possible dupe of the Soviets, gadfly, prophet. He went after Walter Cronkite on camera. His prophecies and muckraking went back like time warps to Periclean Greece, 2,500 years ago. He had a lifelong vendetta against Socrates, of all people.

I wouldn't agree with all of what he said, but Lord knows we need an I.F. Stone these days, and have yet to come up with a worthy successor. I met him three times, which sounds like a morphology of the folktale. But I wish it had been four. He may have taken money from some bad people. Whether he did or not, he set admirable standards of distrust.

Stone came to the Boston University campus in 1974 on the eve of his full "retirement" as an independent journalist. He'd given up I.F. Stone's Weekly three years before, after ill health made him abandon that intrepid little periodical. The circulation of 70,000 had influence far beyond the immediate reach of its subscribers. If you've seen the documentary, you'll remember Izzy stuffing those mailings himself, at the mailbox which must have been the one at the corner of Glenbrook Drive and Macomb Street, Northwest DC. Already in his mid-sixties at the time, with eyeglass lenses the width of hockey pucks, Stone seemed ready to say farewell to his public. But an undergrad got approving laughs in the hall when he asked, "What are your plans for the future?"

Stone charmed by saying, "Well you know, I never did get my B.A., so I was thinking of going to school and studying the classics." The large crowd hooted at this coy bluff, but actually he meant it. His next febrile years would yield his last scoop, *The Trial of Socrates*, published in 1979. I don't think he expected the question at B.U. that day. I know the audience didn't expect his answer.

Stone had a voice dripping in irony, and sounded like W.C. Fields. After I moved to Washington some years later, I went on a warm spring afternoon to the MacArthur cinema before it became a CVS pharmacy. They were showing a grade B Soviet film, and I went because I'd never seen one. Once in the theater, I noticed there were no more than six or seven people in the audience. The film was pretty crappy, and had elements of science fiction, with dinosaurs and space ships. I can't find any reference to it in lists of Soviet movies of the time.

Stepping into the blinding sun from the afternoon's divertissement, I saw a member of the audience fumbling with a pay phone at the nearby gas station. He couldn't see the coins in his hand, and had to feel around the edges to see if they were dimes or quarters.

"Mr. Stone, may I assist you in any way?" I asked. This sturdy little man was trying to call his wife for a ride home, but he took my offer and let me drive him to his house, a few blocks away. He invited me in for lemonade and an hour's chat, and signed over a copy of his 1978 book *Underground to Palestine*. A few house moves later and a little discolored from mold, the book still stands on my shelf. The inscription says, "To Dan Whitman in gratitude, from I.F. Stone, Washington, DC, 5/7/83." Stone probably didn't expect to meet me again, but he did want me to know his views on Palestine.

A couple of years later I was working for something called Delphi Research Associates. Like Voltaire's version of the Holy Roman Empire, it was neither Delphic, nor did much research go on there, but it was made up of associates. Walking to work one morning, I crossed Stone on the Connecticut Avenue sidewalk and stopped to say hello. He smiled affably when I reminded him of the drive home and the Soviet movie a couple of years before. "Yeees…" he said in his W.C. Field cadences, "That film about a dinosawwwr… and a boy who loved him." Stone remembered the film as schlock. "What are you doing these days?" he asked, and I tried to describe. "Delphi!" he frowned. "The Oracle of Delphi. Sold secrets to the Persians." He turned away in disgust, and I never saw him again.

All governments, all authority, were suspect in his eyes. Alone, he unmasked possible fraud in Lyndon Johnson's Gulf of Tonkin Resolution in 1964. Having no "sources" in any government department, he used only the Library of Congress for his sleuthing, and went about matching contradictory statements on the record. He ambushed Walter Cronkite once at a cocktail party when he knew the video camera was running: "So, Walter, what do you think of this Gulf of Tonkin nonsense? Bunch of crap, wouldn't you say, Arthur?" Cronkite tried to inch away, but Stone pursued him: "Surely crap, don't you think, Walter? Yes? No?" It's the only time I ever saw Cronkite lose his cool on camera and hide for cover.

If Stone had friends, he didn't cultivate them. He went by a principle which more journalists and diplomats might adopt: "Believe nothing of what you hear, and only half of what you see." His own near blindness probably worked to his advantage in perfecting skepticism.

Going backwards in time, I relive the lecture series Stone gave in 1979 after the publication of his book on Socrates. He despised Socrates for weakening the Athenian state just for a matter of fastidious self promotion. Gaston Hall was the place to be that fall for his series of three talks. Tickets were being scalped for steep prices. Like *"l'Affaire"* in the 1910s in Paris, the Stone lectures were merely referred to as "The Lectures – have you been?" And if you hadn't at least made the effort to be there, you were dropped from friends' lists. I did attend one.

I go in reverse chronological order for a reason: I.F. Stone worked that way. He took on a controversy from 399 BC, and invented a new genre which still goes without a title – "retrospective prophesy," you might call it. Stone largely ignored the future, and expected little from it. He would surely have been appalled at the Truthism and special effects we live by today. Even the agile humorists who live by the hypocrisy of others.

"No friend but the Truth," I think he would say. "And don't take anyone's word for it, even and especially not Mr. Truth, the odious Socrates."

Truth seeks friends still, but lurks as a feral dog in the alley, living by tossed scraps from reluctant donors.

Amazing Grace and… a Touch of Vodou

May 9, 2011

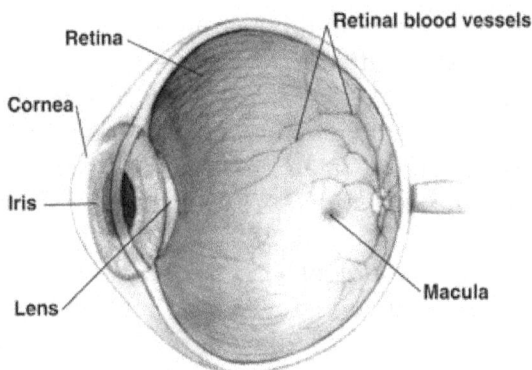

February 29, 2004, Jean Bertrand Aristide fled Haiti as rebels advanced on Port-au-Prince. The same day in Washington, I came down with a nasty fever. A week later I was one hundred percent blind, with a fifteen percent chance of recovery in the right eye only. Coincidence, you might say.

Disclosure: early in 2001, as spokesman for the U.S. Embassy in Port-au-Prince, I contradicted Aristide on Haitian radio as instructed and permitted by my bosses. It had to do with rectifying a point of fact. The night of March 5, Molotov cocktails came over the wall to my quarters in the Turgeot neighborhood of the capital. I guess it was meant as a lesson, but with these things I am a slow learner.

The day of Aristide's departure in 2004, I watched with Haitian expat friends in Washington as the drama unraveled leading to his ouster. That same night I knew something was off. Monday morning I made it to work, but took the rest of the day in bed. Wednesday things began to look cloudy, and by Friday I had no sight at all. The fever wouldn't break. Doctors didn't want to lower the temperature with meds, as that would introduce a variable and make it harder to get a real diagnosis. My eyes burned in their sockets, and something called angle collapse resulted. Imagine a romantic evening with chestnuts in the fire, but consider it from the point of view of the chestnut.

In the unlikely event this should ever happen to you, have a Princess phone in the room: after a week in bed I felt my way around the buttons on the phone, and dialed 411 for a taxi to the emergency ward. Imagine the thirst if you should ever, pardon the expression, burn in hell. And imagine Satan himself telling you, "No water, it might lead to a false thermometer reading."

If the ophthalmologist ever looks in your eye and says, "Oh wow," this is not likely to bring good news. If he calls all the residents on duty to come over and have a look, you can count yourself cooked. The docs all along K Street puzzled over the anomaly, and sent me to the parasitologist, the rheumatologist, the immunologist, the cardiologist, the oncologist. I think they had support group meetings to keep up their own morale in the case. CT scanners whirred and blood labs spun. Medical doctors become very disconcerted if they cannot even name the condition they're dealing with.

I had out-of-range Westergren — whatever that is — and absolute Monocytes. The Neutrophils didn't look proper, and iron, at 20, was perilously low. The good news was that my mediastinal structures appeared normal, and there was no pleural effusion. Hey, take gifts wherever you can find them. Three weeks later, I received a statement in the mail. I couldn't read it at the time, but it said, "Blood culture positive for Alpha Hemolytic Strep," something I was told could lead to, well, death. No hard feelings at this late date for the late delivery.

Months later, the rheumatologist admitted that after he'd seen me, he was creeped out and wanted to wash his hands many times. He had said to me at the time, "We think it's a virus." I countered, "We both know that you say 'virus' when you have no idea of what's going on." He admitted this and we had a good laugh.

You can learn from adversity, it yields useful information. First, you find out quickly who your real friends are. Second, pain trumps despair, and may actually be a remedy for it. Third, if nature's toolbox of intimidation does not overtake you at a time like this, then other forms of it are not likely to do so later in life.

The optic nerve had a field day, trying to pull in data but bringing only trash – graffiti passing by at the speed of an uptown express train, the rose window of Chartres, fish doing backwards cartwheels. Gorgeous images, if false. I now want to thank my optic nerve, publicly, for its valiant efforts those first few days.

People found out about my predicament, and called from different continents to say they would "pray" for me. I didn't know exactly what this meant, but I accepted all offers. Laser treatments pierced the iris so the liquids could find their proper balance in that squishy organ. Well, both of them. Haitian friends asked my permission to look into the causes of this clearly Vodou-caused incident. Russian friends said, "Eat blueberries."

One cold day I was wandering on K Street with my starter sunglasses and cane, trying to find a medical lab. I couldn't see a damn thing. I walked into a wall. A kind soul came out of nowhere and said, "So where did you really want to go?" He directed me to a door. I thought, "Kindness on K Street! This must be what it's like to be a pretty girl!"

What was the meaning of all this, if any? My Haitian friends told me the healing "Right Hand" of Vodou was hard at work, in combat against the harming "Left Hand." They said they had identified the perpetrator, a foreigner living in Port-au-Prince at the time. What do I know?

The rheumatologist said, "OK, we give up. What do you think you've got?"

"Vodou?" I said, and he admitted that all the sages of K Street had come up with no better explanation.

Gradually I got better. One afternoon in late May I entered the National Cathedral as instructed by my praying friends, and saw the actual colors from the stained glass windows. You can't imagine such richness. And so, there goes the still unsolved mystery of a touch of blindness. Haitians, they say, are 70 percent Catholic – and 100 percent Vodou. After a decade of debate, the editors of the Associated Press decided that Vodou was not a superstition but a religion, and gave it the correct spelling and a capital "V" in their style book.

Read into this what you will. The whole adventure might have been a matter of blueberry deficiency. On the powers and perceptions of Haitians, and their extreme kindness, more later.

Pax Vobiscum Alex

May 18, 2011

It will take some doing to get used to a world without Alex Almasov. He died last Friday the Thirteenth, of causes I don't know about, but I don't suppose it matters. He was sixty-something.

Alex was born to a Russian family in Buenos Aires. Figure those two maternal languages, plus his American English picked up along the way. Later in his career, he learned perfect Polish, then Japanese which became the language of the house after he married Yumiko. He was assigned as our trainer at the U.S. Information Agency when 24 of us came in as a "class" in early 1985. In USIA we were Junior Officers in Training (JOTs), and we dealt with things called AmParts, AmSpecs... Uninitiated friends would tell us, "With those jots and specs and parts, you must be very small people."

Imagine the stomach butterflies of 20- and 30-something JOTs coming into a pretty mysterious federal agency, bound for God-knows-where in the Foreign Service, and — for all we knew — asked to leave any personal values and ethics at the door on the way in, though they never said so. The United States has no official feeder institute to train FSOs, and less so for the now extinct USIA, which was melded in the Department of State in 1999.

Acronyms, org charts, crash courses in world culture. We all meant well and wanted to do good by doing well. We were children of the 1960s and '70s.

Alex was the lodestar we went by, our sort of homeroom teacher. We met daily in the sub-basement across the street from 301 Fourth Street SW, in a low-ceilinged, dusty room we called the "Bat Cave." The understated Alex guided us like a taciturn Buddha, signaling with body language when we were on the right track to something, gazing with unaccusing blankness when we didn't get it.

He brought in plenty of speakers during our ten weeks together. Some were better than others. Too many came with a presumptive intimacy, coaching us about something called "corridor reputa-tion," a highfalutin sort of gossip which randomly made and un-made people's careers. I decided from the start to ignore people's judgments of others. Later as an assigning officer, I was well served by this simple principle.

Alex brought the cleverest and the less clever to brief us, but no one came close to him as a solid source of what this profession was all about. We made our various judgments of the smorgasbord, but he never revealed any of his own. This may be the essence of a master teacher.

One morning during our eighth "corridor reputation" spiel, I turned to the classmate next to me, and said, "You'd think they were teach-ing us to be brain surgeons." Mind you, this was five years before people used computers. My classmate found this funny, and I now propose that this was the moment of conception of my single con-tribution to world culture: the expression "It ain't brain surgery," and its variant, "It's not rocket science." You can dispute my claim, but you can't disprove it.

Alex sensed our anxieties but never fed them. He informed and encouraged. He either liked us a lot or faked it very well.

Into the fourth week of training, we were all in angst over the question of whether as press and culture officers we might one day be asked to lie for our country. As good Americans, we always took with a grain of salt what our own government said in public. Had we signed ourselves over to Mephistopheles just for a few thrills and foreign adventures? We each stewed alone, and didn't yet know one another well enough to discuss this dark topic.

How do I know it touched all of us? Because one of the 24 had the gall to broach the topic out loud once, and the fever broke in a minute. The one comment led to another, and another. None of us was purely pleased with U.S. policies we would be expected to understand and explain overseas. None of us was exempt from a sense of dilemma.

"Oh, you mean that one?" Alex said with a twinkle in his eye, and put down his pencil. He knew the moment would come, but dealt with it only after someone verbalized it. Happily, no other speaker was present at that session.

"First, in case you hadn't realized: journalists abroad are not particularly interested in your personal opinion, they just want your help in getting the information. The good scribe wants the statement from Washington. Your own take on it may amuse, but it's not part of the story."

Then in his steady pace, Alex guided us through the options before us: if there is a region in the world where we especially don't like U.S. policy, well then, avoid serving in that region, there are plenty of others. Second, if you dispute a policy, see about effecting a change from within the bureaucracy. Third, the position is not a prison sentence. You can resign at any time.

The relief in the Bat Cave was palpable that morning; the low ceiling seemed to lift. By logic alone, we knew Alex was right; we just hadn't thought or talked it through. Yes, we would give it our best try, without abnegating our precious selves. Alex had been through this, the instances of friction between integrity and loyalty. He had made his own peace with it. We mostly did as well from that moment on, and stayed on through Irangate, the Sandinista-Contra struggle in Central America, the Grenada invasion, and the sordid dealings and ultimate arrest of Manuel Noriega in Panama. We stayed on because we thought we could do more good than harm as Foreign Service Officers. Maybe we did.

Toward the end of the training, other compelling questions mounted. The main one of course was, Where would our postings be? Alex knew in each case, but wasn't allowed to tell us ahead of time. I had a number of hardship posts on my bid list, but really wanted to start out in Milan or Copenhagen. One day after class a few of us were asking Alex about sending cars overseas. He answered the question by the book, then turned to me with his unrevealing smile and said, "In your case, Dan, I'd just wait to get to post first, then get a Volvo locally." We both knew Danes don't make cars.

Message received, and a week less of teeth gnashing, thanks to Alex's enlightened and loving treatment of his disciples. There won't be many more Alex Almasovs.

Mission Possible in Munich

May 20, 2011

Pictured here is Elisabeth Ramzews with an "unaccompanied minor," in Munich, Germany. To Elisabeth's left is the Togolese girl's mother, moments after the two were reunited in 2007, after Elisabeth got the child off the plane that was deporting her. The authorities who had ordered the deportation thanked Ramzews and her Evangelical mission for clearing the record and setting the case straight. Lots of disputes, but an outcome that pleased all.

In recent weeks, President Obama has moved immigration back to the front burner of U.S. policy, approaching yet another third rail in domestic U.S. politics and passions. There could be lessons to learn from the country which created social security in the nineteenth century under a reluctant but savvy Otto von Bismarck.

Germany has one of the highest proportions of properly documented refugees of any country, ranking at the top near Sweden. Not ignoring the country's misdeeds in the twentieth century, Germany finds a way forward in this dilemma-mined issue. There may be a measure of expiation here, but good sense is also a large part of the equation.

Some stats here, from the UN High Commissioner on Refugees: 2005, the last year with published figures, Germany was the first ranking OECD country to take refugees, with 0.7 percent of their population in this category. The United States, by comparison, had 0.4 percent. France, Canada, UK, and the United States have high figures on immigration, but not on refugee intake.

In terms of demand, refugee seekers apply in greatest numbers to the United States, then to France, Germany, Sweden, Canada. In 2010, the numbers of applications to Germany swelled by 49 percent. These are the numbers of those wanting in, not those who got that status.

Not many nations love their government, and Germans are not enamored of theirs. Yet public-private partnerships get set up to take on the challenges of current demographic storms which Western countries will somehow have to face.

Few people favor large movements of refugees, sometimes least of all the refugees themselves. Wide ranges of motivations get them from areas of conflict to countries that are equipped to absorb them – from opportunism to family reunification to survival. Wealthy countries don't seek immigrants, though in aging populations, the source of labor can be welcome.

Elizabeth Ramzews describes herself as a "Delta Force commando" in the complexities and always slipping nuances of theory and practice by the German state toward refugees. When she began to be involved in this field for the Evangelical Church (she herself is Catholic), many of the refugees making their way to her country came from conflict zones in Afghanistan and Iraq. Let that point stand on its own.

Here's how it works in Germany: the State regulates intake, and standardizes the treatment of engagement for "minors separated from their families" (that would be, teenagers between the ages of sixteen and eighteen). But the actual work is conducted by Caritas, its Protestant equivalent Innere Mission, and other NGOs. The State isn't set up to do the work, the NGOs are not set up to pay, so state resources and buildings are given over to the NGOs, with close oversight on how it's working.

At an earlier time, children of the 16-18 range were given a Devil's deal: "Ask for refugee status, and you are then no longer a minor under German law." But this was rectified in 2005.

Ramzews says the relationship between the state and the churches and NGOs is tense, with frequent retracing of the rules of engagement. But the relationship exists. "It is a hard battle, but we are succeeding," she says.

In 1997 the EU instituted the Dublin Agreement, which was meant to set standards for EU treatment of asylum seekers. As of 2001, an application for the EU could be handled by "one, and only one" EU country. The Dublin Agreement says that an applicant's case must be taken up in the country in which the applicant entered – legally or illegally.

In practice, though, some of the points of intake simply do not have systems in place, notably Greece. Hence, word is out in conflict areas that if you want to get out of a war, find a boat going to some shore on the Mediterranean, but then somehow get yourself to Germany, preferably Bavaria. Conditions are not good for the newly arrived, but some NGO will get you a bed and some meals and language lessons, and keep you for ninety days until a real placement can be found. In the meantime, adjudication happens, and some refugees are deported depending on the particulars of their case.

As the U.S. still largely begs off on giving refugee status to individuals fleeing the Iraq and Afghanistan wars, Europe quietly takes up the slack. Many of those coming from Iraq are from ethnic and religious minorities such as Yesidi, Gnostics, Chaldeans, and Mandeans. The latter speak Aramaic, the language of Jesus and John the

Baptist. Chaos in Iraq of course has unleashed old enmities, and the churches and residences of these ancient sects are being targeted increasingly by bombs and killings. So, flee they must.

The Innere Mission center in Munich uses a government-provided facility intended for 30, but now houses 120 – ten to a room. The tenants' situations are not enviable, but they get basic necessities until the courts figure out their next move.

The Munich mission now has 1,800 workers spending time on various social programs dealing with refugees and other social challenges. The national umbrella organization is Diakonie.

It could be that a little less rage, and more pragmatism, might be an alternate approach to the demographic tsunamis we are now dealing with. As we have seen, tsunamis are indifferent to policy, they just happen.

Why is This Man Smiling?

June 4, 2011

We call him Sami; he's our friend in Foggy Bottom. On the good days, he pulls his coffee wagon, trailing behind his car, to the curb at 2100 Virginia Avenue NW, aka "State Annex 3," which sounds like an intergalactic science fiction space vessel.

On Commonwealth Avenue, Boston, in the 1970s, he would have been pushed along out of the way by BU's President Silber. In the Foggy Bottom of today, our national and international bureaucracies know him as a source of light in the penumbra of cubicles and hierarchies of the neighborhood.

Actually he is Musie Tedla, and lives across the bridge in suburban Virginia with his wife and two children. He's from the Horn of Africa, but doesn't get into the particulars of his exact provenance. He never had any dog in the fights of the region. When you ask how long he's been in the U.S., he says only, "Many years."

Wedged between the Pan American Health Organization (PAHO),

the State Department, and a spur of the campus of George Washington University, Sami knows our sidewalk is a good location. Some call the Avenue "Bucharest," because the wide street never developed much traffic to match its expansive girth.

Bureaucrats live atomized lives, but were probably meant to live in villages, like all people. Comunitas gets lost as organizations grow too big. In bureaucracies, messages reach the members through ciphers on a screen. People need tam-tams and musical beats in their lives. They become grumpy without them, like circus animals dressed in tuxedos for the crowd.

WETA music (Schubert, Haydn, de Falla, Villa-Lobos, Ravel...) comes softly out of Sami's little radio from the coffee wagon in the morning. He loves European music. He won't say no if you offer him concert tickets. He'll show up at the concert with his 12-year-old daughter.

People like his smile and hospitality. If you say your name he'll remember it – not to "develop a clientele," but because he has a connection with people. If he hasn't seen you in some weeks, he wants to know where you've been, or if you've traveled.

Anyone wants their half minute with Sami to share the news of the day. If you order the same brew a few times, he will usually say something like, "Caramel chocolate skim macchiato, Ted? Two sugars, then?"

Sometimes the customers don't have all that much in common, especially the PAHO people whose bureaucracy is a mystery to the State Department majority in the neighborhood. But they get in line mainly for the same reasons. The cravings seem to be our equalizer. Weird characters do shuffle along the sidewalk, some of them scary, hearing voices and talking back. They, too, are included if they want to be.

Many say Sami's coffee is the best in Washington. That could be just pride of place. Anyway, we'd probably do the ritual even if it weren't. People will act human if given the chance. It isn't easy when we've over-organized ourselves. The organizations get the "they," and the "we" mixed up.

Maybe I've overstated it: people love the wagon, the coffee, even the ten minutes they spend in line waiting. Sami's wrists know when the pour reaches just above the brim of the paper cup, I don't know how he always gets it right. People's minutes there fortify them for the day, even as the cubicles suck the humanity out.

He works when he's in the mood, and wraps up shop around lunch time or when supplies are down. People who park their cars underground sometimes start the day upstairs by asking around in the office, "Is Sami out there today?" If not, a momentary craving goes unattended and the mood gets soggy. Regardless, people know he'll show up again in a day or two.

When bureaucratic disputes put out toxins in the air, one reliable conflict resolution device at 2100 Virginia Avenue is to say "Let's see if Sami is out there." Those whose style is to walk away from disputes rather than confront them (Type Whatever in the Myers-Briggs test) sneak off for a moment at the coffee wagon. They may just find their antagonists in line for the same reason. The previous harmonies, if any, get reset.

I asked Sami if he had long range plans or wishes. He nodded across the avenue to the D Street entrance of the State Department across the way. The D Street entrance was temporarily blocked for repairs in 2008, and should be reopened in 2012 or 2013. It's really just a door.

Sami said, "I'd just like to serve coffee to everyone in that building over there. Actually, I like coffee."

If Music Be the Food

June 5, 2011

Everyone needs music; no one knows exactly why. There's nothing "universal" about any particular form of it, but people seem to need reminders of their own heartbeat. "Syncopation" of course comes from "syncope," a single, irregular heartbeat sometimes resulting in fainting. Most music has syncopation sooner or later, the point being, I guess, that you can lose the heartbeat for a moment and then get it back. It's reassuring.

In about 1972 I went to Apple Hill, in New Hampshire. I was only visiting. The youngsters there had extraordinary talent, and raised the rafters of a barn with some Haydn and Mendelssohn.

Apple Hill now draws more oldsters than youngsters. In fact, country-wide, there is something happening with sixty-somethings who attend summer music retreats to have another chance at playing well. If they'd been playing at Apple Hill in 1972, they wouldn't be back again now. But there are thousands, maybe more, who show up in the summer, get their name tags, and go to work. They play hard and aim high. They're forgiving of one another's inadequacies, since that's the social glue that makes the process possible.

An amateur is a musician in search of a miracle. Amateurs can achieve miracles for fleeting moments, but aren't usually able to sustain them. If they did, they'd be called "professionals." The fleeting moments are what amateurs live for, their motive for displacement, putting up with communal living and food, and getting corrective advice from maddeningly young and talented coaches. The coaches are heroes. I never met one who was sadistic, or revealed annoyance at hearing screw-ups on the instruments of their expansive souls' yearnings.

I've been to summer music up and down the East Coast. At the end of each of them I say, "No more of this," but then I go back for more. Triumph of hope over experience? It's something we do almost clandestinely, since failure dogs us as the unwanted companion. The mind and heart have their music which the fingers know not.

Something happens as people get together with strangers with a common objective. Forgiveness, I've said, is a part of it. More compelling is the bridge spanning chasms of difference. You can find yourself in a quartet with people with almost nothing in common, but for the single overlapping interest of making music with others. Social phenomena happen, with conversations off the deep end of one's own experience and interests, but with the link of the one interest everyone shares. A contractor, a physicist, a poet, a street person, a teacher can find surprising connections, and might all know the same Villa-Lobos quartet to their surprise. At a recent introductory session, the retired physicist said, "I have a PhD in mathematics but I never learned to count." Good one.

It's like sitting with a stranger on a bus or train. You might talk about things you'd never mention to someone you knew you'd see again for sure.

Now is summer migration season. The last retreat I attended was probably the best, set in idyllic surroundings, the innkeepers supportive and inquisitive. Even the food sustained. Usually the food is the first sacrifice one makes in going to these things, but not this last time.

People got along. A young man with marital issues received attention and free advice from people who'd been through these things themselves. The music itself – well let's not dwell too much on that. The teachers know how to make things better without leading people off the cliff of unreasonable expectations.

A common theme at music retreats is reincarnation. "In my next lifetime I'll just do violin." "I'll be a clarinetist next time." "I'm coming back as a quartet." These become commonplace.

Everyone wants a second chance, either to redo a fudged passage, or a life that could have been lived through different options. I don't hear much discussion of this, but it's a big societal event in a country with lengthening life spans and a belief—despite evidence—in better times ahead.

Coping with Opus

June 5, 2011

I was never exactly alarmed or frightened of Opus Dei, even after reading Dan Brown's ramblings on the subject. I read his *Code* thing only because friends told me I should. I'm trying to remember who told me so. Those were hours I will never get back.

Opus may be a little creepy, but probably not lethal these days. It seems good at taking care of its members. Like most sects, its verbiage will make your eyes glaze over.

The Opus people in Pamplona run the best media training program by far in Spain, at the University of Navarra. As the media official at the U.S. Embassy in Madrid in the early 1990s, I was offered up as lunch partner for the Opus Dei spokesman, the day he decided to cultivate a friendship with the U.S. government. I said, "Do I have to?" The boss said, "Well you're the media guy, and hell if I'm going."

Duty called. Spokesmen speaking to spokesmen seems like a tautology, but that's the way it works. We set a date for the restaurant at the lower level of the Hotel Galgos, on the calle Claudio Coello, two blocks from the embassy. One must make sacrifices for the homeland.

People in Washington made fun of us in Madrid, for never being available at 3:00 in our afternoon for phone calls or satellite video broadcasts. Most of the contact work in Madrid was done over lunch, and lunch happens from 3:00 to 5:00 there. This is real work. You shouldn't envy us, a person can get sleepy to the point of pain over a meal at that hour in a hot climate. Circadian rhythms push a person to siesta at that hour, which of course is the reason for that ancient custom in Iberia. Madrid's current practice of mixing business and lunch in the late afternoon may be more a departure from custom than an extension of it. But I don't make the rules.

So was I eager to get the Opus line that hot spring day? Not at all, but I knew there could be some value in taking up the gauntlet and trying.

I think we started with a tasty cold soup, but that's not the point. I realized from the start that sleep and boredom would be my adversaries that day.

The Opus spokesman was a gentle man and avoided hyperboles in our almost three-hour conversation. I still don't know what the point was of it all, but I did learn that the older an outlying sect becomes, the more soft spoken. Opus, mind you, openly seeks power, and got a big chunk of it in the Vatican when it rescued the Vatican Bank from bankruptcy and vague scandal in the 1980s. If you like these things, google the Banco Ambrosiano and Roberto Calvi, and his "acrobatic suicide" under a bridge in London in 1982.

Back to that day in Madrid. I've found that quoting others while distancing yourself from those quotes is a failsafe tool of publicists. "People say that Opus was friendly with the Franco regime," I said as I poured my partner's wine.

Taking no offense, the Opus man acknowledged those rumors, noted that a foreigner can be forgiven for picking up inaccuracies, then eagerly spent an hour and a quarter refuting them. Opus had suffered more than others under Franco, he insisted. And I hope he got rewards back home for driving the point. I remember my own inner processing of the new information: "I am blessed, I need only catch a few things he's saying, and remember to stay awake. The Angel of Death has spared me once again."

At the same time, I knew I'd need another couple of questions at hand for when the monologue ran out. Incredibly fortunately, I needed only one other: I asked why religions proselytize, since I've never understand why they do so. I still don't, really. If you have a solidly held belief, would it not dilute, rather than strengthen it, to seek to draw in others? I'm not being perverse here, at worst, naïve. Home run. The Opus man loved the question, and spent another 75 minutes answering it. The argument went something like this: when I embrace a belief, I am comforted by having others around me who share it. Fair enough.

Thus I not only survived the experience, but really did learn something of value. Now, twenty years later, I share with you my coping mechanism and the relief I sense even to this day, in summoning the stamina and courage to stay conscious that whole afternoon.
Fact check: of Franco's 116 cabinet ministers in 1936-75, eight were Opus Dei prelates. Whether they were under his thumb or benefiting from the relationship, I will not seek to judge. Pope John Paul II beatified Opus founder Jose Maria Escriva in 1992, and canonized him in 2002. Escriva was politically neutral in public, but did say to a colleague, "Hitler against the Jews, Hitler against the Slavs, this means Hitler against communism." You have to judge people in the context of their times.

Most importantly, if you are fighting sleep but have to order wine, sip slowly and go with the white.

Totentanz at Orly

June 6, 2011

Lots of things happened in 1989. Berlin Wall down, Tiananmen Square, the birth of younger friends.

Not the least was the G-7 Economic Summit in Paris that year, also marking the Bicentennial of the French Revolution. President Mitterrand made a grand show of it, with a type of parade never seen, and which seemed the prototype for the fanciful Barcelona Olympics opening of 1992. Parodies, stilts, artfully unfurled banners, modernized medieval tunes, and, well, the fanfare that became the signature of Mitterrand and his culture minister, Jack Lang. Thirty heads of state flew in for the event.

My task was pretty simple: get the camera angle set up for President George HW Bush's arrival at Orly. The press corps traveled on Air Force One, seated at the rear of the plane. They had to disembark from the aft door and get the cameras in place within about

90 seconds, to photograph the president as he emerged from the forward door.

Pretty simple stuff, it just meant having clear access to the tarmac, knowing where the cameras were to be set, and hustling the press off the rear of the plane. The consequences of failure were, well, unthinkable. Also very unlikely, with all the precautions built in.

I attended the countdown meetings of course. These were stressful for the organizers, but kids' play for us supernumeraries. A couple hundred people crowded into the hotel conference room, coffeed up, and went through the paces in painstaking detail, even as tiny changes were introduced twice daily for the five-day prep. I was lucky to have a lengthy liberal education and a pressed suit. No other qualifications were needed except something like "nimbleness," which is hard to measure until you need it.

As per tradition, untrusting youngsters sent out from Washington had to imagine anything that could go wrong. For them, success meant a possible stint as a White House political appointee someplace, failure meant oblivion. Oblivion is not all that bad, but it's out of style with young people.

They changed my exact scenario a dozen times, I think intentionally for security purposes. You can't have too many people knowing the exact time and location of a president's appearance, so you keep changing it. Not only malfeasance, but also bumbling can introduce variables you don't want. We would seek to control the weather as well for the photo color backdrop, but that part is pretty reliable in Paris in mid-July.

The day the heads of state flew in—one every twenty minutes—I got a taxi out to Orly. Like baseball, VIP work calls for a lot of waiting and then quick precision and actions that are over almost before you notice. I made it to the perimeter gate as planned, wearing my security lapel pin. The pin gave me access everywhere, of course for a limited time. Very sharp minds made up these systems.

I pulled out my sensitive-but-unclassified map of the landing square, to triple check my location. Then I went to the perimeter gate to get inside. For a 90-second period, the publicity for the President of the United States would be my exclusive domain.

I recognized the Secret Service at the gate, from the countdown meetings. Maybe they noticed me as well.

"Can't come in," one said. I thought he was joking, and took a step toward the gate.

"No, really, we can't let you in," he said, eyeballing my security lapel pin. "Your pin's expired." He pointed at his watch and showed how it was eight minutes past the hour of validity of my pin. They changed color and design every hour.

"Well let's see," I said. "I really have to position the White House press to photograph the president on arrival. The plane's due in 45 minutes."

SS wouldn't budge. I understood his dilemma ("no exceptions"), maybe he understood mine. Someone hadn't thought to give me the color pin that would work for the following hour.

"Any way around this?" I asked.
"Sorry, no," he said.

My stomach tightened. I wondered what the Good Soldier Schweik would do.

Ugly scenarios came to mind. Aside from a prematurely snuffed out career, I imagined public humiliation, urban legends and jokes at my expense, an angered president, even a jinxed G-7. I walked outside the airport perimeter, considering the options. There were no good ones. Journalists are clever people, maybe they would position themselves without assistance, get their shot, and move on? Not likely. Everyone knew they follow the rules and limits when someone sets them. But without a pool corral, they would all scuffle for a close-up of the president. It wouldn't take long for the post mortem to nail me as the moron who caused the debacle.

I was pretty rational in my despair, but was able to toggle only between two outcomes: my destruction or my self-destruction. I was pretty sure I'd go with the former, but I did consider the latter. I kept walking, which is the thing to do when you've hit a wall in a maze.

Absorbed with my fantasies and anxieties, I didn't even notice there was another gap in the fence a few dozen meters ahead. I heard, *"Vos papiers!"* and looked up to see a French gendarme at the next entrance. He was solo, and had total authority over his gate. His words to me were an order, a challenge, but also an opportunity.

Possibly he understood the situation, and wanted for us all to get through intact. His neck was the size of a Douglas fir. His massive shoulders and forearms might have killed Bedouins in late colonial wars, or could have.

When backed against a wall, never retreat; it serves no purpose. I dug into my wallet and pulled out my District of Columbia driver's license. It all has to do with the wrist: I presented my DC license to the gendarme and looked straight into his beady eyes.
"Passez!" he said, and waved me through. He might have winked, but I didn't dare look.

I found myself all alone in the Orly *Salle d'Honneur*, then exited the other side to the tarmac just as Air Force One was taxiing to its final position. With not another soul in sight, I advanced under the wing of the plane and suddenly saw the camera angle just as they'd described it at the countdowns. Checking my SBU map one last time, I got to the rear steps of the plane. I made myself visible to the photographers as they hurried down the steps to get into position for their angle for the arrival shot.

The gendarme, a rhinoceros of a man, stood proudly at attention at the gate, his turf.

48

The photographers got their shot, I survived, and highest bureau-cratic achievement was realized: nothing noticeable, nothing out of place.
Anecdotes should have applications. There could be one here: when trapped, keep moving. When stumped, consider the worst options. If you plan to disrupt a VIP appearance, you might get in, but there can be a gendarme to block the exit, ready to break you like a toothpick. Keep a cool head, but be willing to have it ripped from your thorax if you try anything funny.

PD on the House

June 11, 2011

I hear Cole Porter's seven best words, "…and in Boston even beans do it," currently reprised in Woody Allen's recent movie, *Midnight in Paris*.

I refer, of course, to Public Diplomacy, which everyone has discovered in the past ten years, or was it the past ten minutes? The Chinese have caught on late but nimbly, setting up Confucius Centers on the model of the British Council, Alliance Française, and Goethe Institute. The United States has mostly abandoned government-run libraries and culture centers overseas for security and budgetary reasons, but they had a good run for forty years.

Like the centipede stymied by the question of how he walks, organized societies have done public diplomacy from the start, they just never had a name for it.

The occasion for this reflection is the impressive conversion of François Rivasseau to the New Religion. Rivasseau was one of Washington's most skillful diplomats as the deputy chief of mission at the French Embassy. He remains so, as the PD-oriented rep of the European Union Delegation to the United States.

He "came out" June 9 at the Johns Hopkins School of Advanced International Studies, chatting amiably with SAIS's Kurt Volker, a recent U.S. Ambassador to NATO.

A refreshment, really, to have a new colleague starting from a point of perspective over gimmicks, reason over infatuation. This is how the French are at their best, and it is the "love" part of the Franco-American love-hate relationship. American practitioners sometimes seize the bone and leave the meat and… well, as a vegetarian myself, I'll let up on that metaphor.

The Lisbon Treaty took European integration to a new level in 2010, making Cathy Ashton its foreign minister of sorts, and sought to merge 27 diplomacies into one. To do so, and also not do so. I explain: smart Europeans take their ancient cultures and histories and upend them to say "We're only 50 years old," referring of course to the EU. They see America as the "old" democracy, clocking in at 222 years. This is a skillful turn to have Americans open up to the European concept, without antagonizing them. "Welcome," we want to say when they put it this way.

June 9 at SAIS, Rivasseau spoke of America once having been an extension of Europe, with the roles now sometimes reversed. No one loses identity in recognizing this. On religious tolerance, for example, both sides of the Atlantic say they seek the same outcome: live and let live. The Pilgrims, he reminded us, made the perilous ocean crossing to escape state religion, and started out wanting the ties of church and state cut entirely.

"Those of us who were unable to escape," Rivasseau said coyly, "learned to look to the state to prevent abuses of religion. Same objective, different application."

As a newcomer to PD, Rivasseau has quickly deciphered the terms so recklessly misused by some of the self appointed experts: hard, soft, smart power. If you insist on using these loaded terms (it's like "sanction," which can mean two opposites), you ought to know what you're talking about. Go to the source, Joseph Nye, who made them up and defined them pretty clearly. Not everyone needs to know, but many opine. Certificates could be required for those who need to drop these terms. If so, Rivasseau would get one on the first try.

Americans and Europeans tend to bicker; it sort of keeps us going and keeps tourism up. Many of the roles have flipped, as when Germany became a moral compass for America's recent actions in the southern Mediterranean. It used to be the other way around. But Obama and Merkel weren't faking it last week when they affirmed the two nations' abiding friendship. What we've been through!

It's a nice irony to hear a perceptive European talk about "melting pot," "conformity," "identity," "roots," and "leveling process," referring to—surprise!—something other than America. Sophists say, "We are too diverse, you cannot call us 'Europeans' (substitute 'American' or 'African.')" Get over it. We all have multiple identities, and seek a comforting sunset view on anyone's shores.

Americans are famously uneasy with the term "culture," and never tire of redefining it. Europeans just do it. Cole Porter would have said so.

Rivasseau's most engaging factoid was the quote of the late Jean Monnet (creator of the European Coal and Steel Community), who said at the end of his life, "If I had to do it over again, I would take culture, not economics, as the basis of European integration."

As an American myself, I don't know what culture is either. But I "know it when I see it." I've been doing PD and cultural exchange since 1969. I still don't really understand why taxpayers pony up for it, I'm just glad they do. I don't ever want to have to argue the case in a legislative body. J. William Fulbright did that for me, and his arguments have yet to be superseded.

52

So China does it, Europe always did it but now does it collectively. And François Rivasseau has now become one of us. Welcome, François, to our world! Unsolicited advice to the newcomer: let the definers spin themselves out to exhaustion, then remain standing and help us see ourselves from a friendly outsider's perspective, as you did June 9. It's good for our so-called hubris.

Many Would Rescue, Few Would Help

June 18, 2011

This is Mary Lourdes Elgirus. To her friends, of whom I'm lucky to be one, she's Marilou.

June 16. I drove her through a rainstorm in Washington, DC, to the Greyhound terminal where she caught her overnight bus to Boston. This gets her back to Framingham, where she has pitched her tent after six decades of moving around from Haiti to France, Canada, New York, and now Boston. She has what the French call *"bougeotte,"* the need to keep moving. Everyone has the *bougeotte* to a degree, some more than others. Those who act it out do so for different reasons – past deeds, curiosity about the wide world (aka wanderlust), or some unsettled part of themselves. *Bougeotte* in its purest form can be a need to get away from circumstances, or to improve them.

Marilou was senior cultural assistant at the U.S. Embassy in Port-au-Prince in the 1980s and again in the '90s. She was never not mounting eight projects at a time, to widen the horizons of Haitians, and to give Americans a view of her country which took them beyond a confirmation of stereotypes. In this sense she was an educator, and remains so, now at Mass Bay Community College in Framingham. She's carried around her PhD in Education for some twenty years.

She was incommunicado after the earthquake of January, 2010. We who knew her imagined her in a frenzy of activity but in fact, she now says, she was just discouraged. A lot of things have been said about Haiti's misfortunes. I won't add much, I'll just say that collectively, the outsiders were culpable, or at best clumsy. They thought they could beguile Haitians, or show them the way, or Christianize them more thoroughly. In fact they mainly bullied them.

Outsiders seek to "save" Haiti, but few have bothered really to help. Their motives are ego, misery tourism, checking a spiritual box, or of course financial gain. Even now you can turn a buck in Haiti. In the worst of times the Barbancourt will still flow. Compassion usually is embedded among other motives, but has become layered like Schliemann's Troy.

Americans in particular lack the staying power to survive a problem once they see that it can't be solved. One admirable exception is Sean Penn. There are some others.

Of course Haiti is now a living laboratory of the failed state, the example of what you become when 98 percent of your forests are destroyed, and the consequences of dismantling a corrupted but efficient *latifundia* system of production, for the benefit of social justice. Outsiders now express tempered optimism for the energy and motives of the new president, Michel Martelly. And why shouldn't they, when any change from his predecessors would be an improvement.

Marilou left Haiti during the Namphy times of the late 1980s, and stayed out during the Coup period when the high-hatted generals took over in the 1991. Then with many others, she returned when it seemed Jean Bertrand Aristide would put his rhetorical prowess and considerable energies and charm to the benefit of his people. He didn't.
She always had a foot in New York, another in Montreal. She stuck

it out in Port-au-Prince to see what she could do to improve her country. She adopted children, now speaks of "my grandchildren." Working ten-and twelve-hour days at the embassy on cultural and educational exchange, in her "spare time" she also set up something called the Martin Luther King Center for Peace. She got a small building donated for the cause, and some giveaway furniture. Gary Lissade, the very capable Justice Minister at the time, helped inaugurate it in early 2001.

Marilou overcame discouragement a thousand times, then made it as far as Framingham in 2005. She never really "left" Haiti, and goes back often.

The rainstorm let up at around 6:30 the other day at the Greyhound station. Marilou had been in Washington at a conference on Haiti. She had her return plane ticket, but couldn't afford the $700 change fees, when she'd been called back early for the sudden funeral of a great aunt in Boston. Her overnight bus fare was 62 dollars.

The DC Greyhound terminal never exactly captured the majesty or romance of travel at its best, but now it has fallen on shockingly decrepit times. Maybe 20 travelers meandered through the vast, empty hall. A young man positioned beneath a sign saying "Express Tickets" explained how bus tickets are no longer sold at the counter, only at the computerized screens.

Marilou showed the cane she walks with, now that her knee troubles her. "And what if I had crippled hands, would you help me at the computer screen?" she asked. The young man didn't say much, but was clear he wouldn't help.

Greyhound once attracted European tourists who felt they could discover America by reliable surface transport, meeting the vox populi along the way. Now the Bolt Bus, Chinatown Express, and others bring cheaper options that all the young people use. Why had Marilou stuck with a Greyhound so sadly in decline?

She lives by her values. At the moment of the snapping of this picture, she said, "*Je suis traditionaliste!*"

Herodotus of Arlington, Virginia

June 18, 2011

Charles Stuart Kennedy interviews retired diplomats. I mean, really interviews them. He's done 48 hours with Tom Pickering alone, the George Kennan of our time – and says he hasn't even gotten yet from Pickering's childhood into his Foreign Service career.

Americans have multiple careers. Stu has had only two, but they total 55 years. He was consular officer in the Department of State for 30 years, starting in Frankfurt in 1955 as a refugee officer. He went to Saigon, Naples, Athens, Belgrade, Ankara and beyond.

When he "retired" in 1986 he started interviewing colleagues. Trained earlier in history at Williams College, he got a cassette recorder and threw questions at colleagues and contacts, at first something like a journalist. Then after a year or so, he set to developing a methodology. He did it solo over the years, and turned it into a way of registering a cross section of American society. Women and minorities, he noticed, came into a field previously reserved mainly for the pale, male and Yale. They all had stories to tell. Nothing against Yale.

The number of stories that have gone through Stu's head and eyes and ears is staggering. Among over a thousand he interviewed, 50 died just last year alone. "Get them before they die," is one of his mottos. Seventeen hundred of them—most done by Stu, some by others—are on the Library of Congress website, something like constellations in the heavens. They call it the "cloud" these days, but eternity goes farther.

Stu has his strong preferences, but always gives room to others'. If you've met this man, you started learning things from about the time you met him.

His interviews go back to the 1980s, but contain eyewitness references to times as far back as the 1920s. The topics include normal places everywhere, plus conflicts and drama in World War II, Korea, Vietnam, Grenada, Central America, Colombia, China, Malaysia, Serbia, Bosnia, Kosovo, Algeria, Afghanistan, Iraq, and Israel-Palestine. He interviewed a Foreign Service Officer who played dead on the tarmac in Jonestown, Guyana, and a GI who parachuted into a flooded field in France during the Normandy invasion. Carrying his typewriter over his head to keep it dry, the GI brought in "the first combat typewriter into occupied Europe."

At a lunch June 16 honoring his 25 years doing oral histories, Stu said the collection was a "miracle." He doesn't get into false modesty, but nor does he ever take all the credit for anything. "Behind every miracle there is someone making the miracle happen," he said. Nobody has counted the pages of transcripts on the website, but it can't be fewer than a quarter of a million.

The organization behind him, the Association for Diplomatic Studies and Training, was founded at about the same time Stu started interviewing, but the two got together a bit later.

Stu talks about a "wasting asset," the 600 interviewed over the years who have already now "passed to that Great Chancery in the sky." That's over a third of the collection. He did manage to get them in time.

58

A lot of people love this guy. He got their stories out of them, the one thing nearly everyone is eager to give. Many want to be asked, but never realize it until someone does so.

What do you do with eyewitness history? Keep it. Someone will need it sooner or later. People don't go looking for it, but many have been amazed when they suddenly needed it and found it was already there.

After 25 years at this work (plus his 30 years in the consular corps), Stu says he sees three themes in the 1,700 posted interviews. Time to listen up! 1. The growing roles of women and minorities over the years; 2. The accomplishments of diplomats during the Cold War ("If diplomats hadn't done their job, we would be living in caves or not here at all."); and 3. The emerging story of the United States as "the indispensable nation." Stu is not a flag waver and doesn't trust those who are. But he sees the U.S., still, as "the world's nanny." "If the U.S. wasn't pushing things, who the hell would be doing it?"

Note to reader: catch and hold rhetorical questions from people who've been at it for 55 years. There aren't that many left.

Now go see the site: http://memory.loc.gov/ammem/collections/diplomacy/

Looking into the Sun

June 20, 2011

The GWOT (Global War on Terror, R.I.P.) seemed to some to be the last Good War. We recaptured some of our RPGs from the early 1980s, then sent in MRAPs, dodged IEDs, had TTXs at NDU and established FOBs in the field. Our ROE became liberalized, permitting us to engage with AQIM in the Sahel. TSCTP took notice. The DO across the river gave us some inroads and PsyOps evolved to MISO. And as Napoleon said, "an army travels on its MREs." We had our share of PTSD in our AOR, but the MO was to rely on PRTs as guided and coordinated by JFCOM.

It was a good decade for acronyms. The cause was certainly just: to contain crazed zealots, kill them when possible, keep them on the run, and erode the support they had in their popular base. We had zealots too, but they didn't target non combatants in the GWOT, while the other side did.

Then a curious thing happened: in about 2006 the GWOT morphed into something called the War of Ideas. We would engage with the same tactics as our adversaries, only for a different cause. There was a lot of internal discussion about this phrase, though I doubt people around the world noticed or cared much. The politico man who created the term said publicly that he was uncomfortable with it, but added that we, his colleagues, could come up with nothing better. This was not entirely true.

Nobody liked the notion of "ideas" as an instrument of war, and we gave a couple dozen options at an afternoon meeting on the State Department's seventh floor. The creator of the phrase, wedded to it for some reason, wrote down our other suggestions on a legal pad but didn't use any of them. He later claimed in an op/ed that we hadn't even suggested them.

We were instructed to "engage" with Muslims wherever we found them in the field, and to throw Iftaar dinners at our embassies to break the Ramadan fast together. This was your near equivalent of having the Saudi ambassador invite you over for Christmas or for your own communion (shouldn't it have been the other way around?) but the idea caught on and people discovered one another with delight over Iftaar dinners.

Still, we approached Muslims (whom we feared) and tried to distract them from the murderous tendencies we suspected they had, by assuring them that we neither feared nor suspected them. It wasn't altogether believable, but the food was good, and we enjoyed one another.

It came to me in Mali that we were going about this all wrong. I attended the best cultural event I've ever witnessed, which was Public Affairs Officer Mary Speer's exhibition of Koranic illustrated manuscript remakes, done by women in Timbuktu to evoke—but not imitate—the originals from the fourteenth century versions in libraries in that ancient seat of learning.

Mali is ninety percent Muslim. Mary invited all the imams in the country, and I think all of them came. Many came up to her individually and said in hushed tones, "Thank you for sparing us the usual Christian-Muslim palaver. These art works inspire us."

Hence, what I call "looking at the sun." If you look directly, you'll burn your eyes and cause permanent damage. If you engage with a person on a topic obliquely other than the obvious one between you, and sail off to attention points of another stripe, it will actually bring you closer together. No eye damage, there.

Don't say, "Tiger, Tiger burning bright," if you want to befriend the tiger. Say, instead, "Tiger, let's have a drink and see what we might do together of interest."

Mary Speer was never much exalted in her system for catching the spirit, but she should have been.

Ten Out, Ninety to Go

June 22, 2011

Stop the presses, did the Commander-in-Chief really just say this? Ten thousand out this year, 23,000 more by 2012 until the surge is out? That will leave 70,000 until 2014.

"But what could he have meant by this?"

That's a quote, but not by Beck, Olbermann, or Blitzer. It's attributed to Otto von Bismarck May 17, 1838, the day his rival and colleague Charles Maurice de Talleyrand died. Talleyrand survived as France's foreign minister through Louis XIV, the Revolution, Napoleon I, Louis XVIII, Charles X, and Louis-Philippe. Talleyrand cared unequivocally for his cause (France) but was a shark among others.

Did Bismarck mean to say that a leader dies more often than he tells the truth?

"Withdrawal in summer of 2011 – calamity!" said some in 2009 and 2010. Joe Biden, Aaron to Obama's Moses, said in effect, "He didn't say withdrawal, he said 'beginning of withdrawal.'" Many didn't think—shocked!—that a politician might say what he meant, or do what he said. Bob Gates came to the rescue two weeks ago in a speech in Brussels: "I can tell you there will be no rush to the exits."

A recent Pew Research Center poll said that more than half of Americans want a decrease of U.S. troops in Afghanistan, regardless of whether Karzai's Afghanistan can make a go of it or not.

A CBS poll conducted last week showed, too, that 64 percent want a decrease. There is even aisle-crossing on this. All figures are up, except our nation's solvency and ability to put up a billion more dollars every 72 hours.

In any case we know from our Walter Lippmann, from nine decades ago, that opinions have the lifespan of a mayfly. Decisions, though, stay on the books until someone decides they are mistakes.

President Obama's decision in this case will please no one entirely, but it is the sum total of Cato non-interventionists, Heritage exceptionalists, Pelosi let's-get-going-ists, McCain determinationists, and Kerry prudentialists.

On the eve of the Normandy invasion, the Supreme Allied Commander in Europe would have been nuts to announce the GPS coordinates of the landing, but he said clearly it would happen, and everyone knew he meant it. He also told the troops he trusted them to prevail. Imagine, a president (Ike or Obama) repeatedly making a promise, then actually keeping it.

Not to deify the man, but sheesh, we haven't had it this good in a long time.

The Case for Aid

June 26, 2011

June 23, House Majority Leader Eric Cantor (R-VA) pulled out of the U.S. budget negotiations. The same day, Liberia's president had the pluck to go to the Hill to argue the case for sustained foreign aid. Unenviable.

Ellen Johnson Sirleaf, Liberia's 24th president, is the first elected female Head of State in Africa. Well, even being elected makes her something of a *rara avis*.

From the Hill she came to the Center for Global Development in the Dupont area, and chatted on mic with CGD's capable V.P. for Programs, Todd Moss.

And appropriately so. CGD wages a lonely battle seeking to demonstrate that foreign aid can work. Lots of people disagree. The Center launched Charles Kenney's book last spring, a cheerful opus called *Getting Better: Why Global Development is Succeeding and How We can Improve the World Even More* (New York: Perseus, 2011).

President Johnson looked a little worn out after her transatlantic flight and a session on the Hill all on the same day. But there was love in the room at Dupont, and she heightened it with her understated determination and gentle irony. At one point she demurred on a technical question about microcredit, and picked out her finance minister in the audience to answer the query. It seems she trusts her staff.

The national budget for Liberia is $350 million. Well aware of the world she lives in, she said, "You could hardly run a school district here for that much."

No whining, however! Johnson went on the record to say Liberia will be free of need for foreign aid by the year 2020. And that the country would get out from under its debt by 2030. While bold, these were not wild assertions: studies and time lines indicate that it is possible.

In the five years she has been Liberia's president, Johnson has come from post conflict to direct foreign investment of $16 billion. When oil was discovered in Liberia some months ago, she went straight to the Norwegians for a primer on how to avoid the "oil curse," and to learn how to require foreign investors to put Liberians to work, with hospitals and schools in the deal.

If we say "one of the twenty fastest growing economies in the world," we remember of course from whence Liberia comes. Still, with the caveats, Johnson cites this accomplishment with muted pride, and assures that her country is "poised for take-off." All is economics, with her luckless people now the beneficiaries. She turns to the Liberian diaspora of 300,000 in the United States to be the start-up market for T-shirts reversing their usual pattern to go from a poor country to a rich one. Not a bad tactic.

How can the United States help further? Never mind the M-16s or innovative postage stamps. "Help us rebuild a damaged hydro-dam," she said.

Are the Chinese taking over? "They like big footprints…We have no China fear." We'll take their hospitals and public works projects, she said in effect, but we are "with the West."

Will there be an "African Spring" to match the one in the Middle East? "We already had ours," she said. "We had our military dictatorships, and we have moved beyond."

It seemed from the moments when the president best overcame travel fatigue, the single point she meant most to drive home was that foreign aid is working in Liberia, and that the current level of growth was possible only thanks to outside help. "Graduation" is within sight. Imagine getting T-shirts from an oil-rich country!

President Johnson drew a tough assignment in the debating team: it's in our own interest to keep foreign aid up, even during a time of U.S. budget Gotterdammerung. It doesn't look good, with a thousand false starts. But if the "African Spring" has already passed, then it's time to keep it up and finish the job. [Ed. comment: what did we expect, backing turkeys all those years?]

So it might be a bad time to be asking, but the question has an implied answer: "Help awhile longer, and your own markets will expand."

One questioner asked Johnson why there were so few female leaders in Africa. She ran the numbers quickly in her head and said, "Considering who the candidates are for your 2012 elections, it seems Liberia is at least eleven years ahead of you."

Then she stepped into the crowd and we all lined up for drinks.

The Importance

June 27, 2011

I'll call him Leonard. Actually his name is Earnest. Not that it is, but I'm calling him Ernie.

I worked with Ernie and hold him in high esteem. Others don't, and say he had improper relations three years ago with a woman who received U.S. government funds from him to do a civil society project. Ernie's grant to her was for an amount that would have kept a C-130 in the air for seven to ten seconds.

The "grantee" has filed an affidavit asserting that, as a lesbian, she wouldn't have bedded Ernie. She is suing the U.S. government for damages in canceling a contract retroactively, after she completed the work. No one disputes that the terms of the contract were met, and that her final reports were on time and more than complete. If she wins her lawsuit against the government, it will cost us ten times the amount of the grant itself. If she loses, it will still cost five times the amount. Ernie's accuser, also a woman, has admitted that the grantee hit on her, and has signed a statement saying so. In effect, she recanted her own accusation from three years ago.

Lesbians do lapse on occasion, so Ernie could be, well, louche in the eyes of the system.

Care for more of this? The government has decided to prove a negative, and has pulled Ernie from his current posting after ten months of expensive language training. It has also told him to re-tire, though he doesn't want to. ("She says you didn't, and you say you didn't, but still you might have.")

A lot of stuff goes on with us hominoids below the belt, likely more goes on in the mind that thinks below the belt. It does seem there were some factory defects in our design, and someone other than the Designer is going to pay for it. I don't know how to quantify these things, but some government officials are planning to do so, in this case and hundreds of others.

Newspapers are carrying lists these days of public officials who have done naughty and even disgusting things. The difference, I think, is that these officials have said "I have no sinning organs as far as I know, but if I do I certainly never put any of them to use."

Not so with Ernie. Both of the accused say they would like a chance to answer the charges, but there aren't any really. I'm not an expert on Ernie's private life, but I think a lot of other people aren't either. Meanwhile he is being hounded out of a job.

I do know he did his work, because I saw him do it.

There is nothing funny about people being led where they wish not to go. It should not happen. Nor, however, with people pushing the "accuse" button lightly, when it costs someone's livelihood. Let me overstate it to make a point: this is Stalinism without the bullets. Stalin at least never maintained the conceit of picking his victims according to a set of written rules. Give him credit at least for that. I am a taxpayer and I want my money back.

I am not saying that the half million dollars already spent on this single matter would balance our budget. But does this profligacy work for you? Imagine how many Oreo cookies we could distribute to kids in the desert for this amount.

Idle comparisons between military hardware that costs real money, and civilian activities that further our interests, don't impress me. The line items are different in scale and nature. But the little Stalins settling accounts at my expense do not impress, either. They're doing it every week. In one department alone, there is a backlog of 300 cases. Lawyers say that 90 percent of them go in favor of the individual when they make it to court.

The government will win or lose this case, and the thousands of others which stand in the docket at this time. But the only guaranteed loser in these prosecutions is me. I want my Oreos and I want them now. Not for me, but for the kids in the desert who wouldn't know a tort if it hit them in the face. Let Ernie go, please, and let's get on with business.

When Slava Met Yo-Yo

June 28, 2011

June 28, 2011. Dateline Washington. Slow news day. "Limits on video games," "President waging charm offensive," "Bachmann, Blagojevich…" zzzzzzz.

Harp music, image fades… flash back to 1976. Spring is in the air and we're seated in the balcony section of Sanders Theater in Cambridge, Mass.

Yo-Yo Ma was pre-med at Harvard in those days. He hadn't yet admitted to being a cellist, but a lot of us in Cambridge went to hear him in the neighborhood college houses, and we knew this young talent would break through onto the world stage sooner or later.

Mstislav Rostropovich was still completely a cellist back then, hadn't yet taken over the conductor's baton. He had made it out of the USSR, but wasn't exactly an American citizen yet. You were a fool if you passed up an opportunity to hear him play, which he did tirelessly and often, only moving around a lot and hard to chase down.

The announcement of a Rostropovich master class went by town crier back in those pre-Facebook days, and a couple hundred of us got wind that Yo-Yo would be one of the players.

It was like an immense practical joke on Rostropovich. He was the only person in the packed house who didn't know yet about Yo-Yo. The latter still belonged only to us, we who knew him and sat with him in coffee houses on Dunster Street and Winthrop, and encouraged him to take the plunge and let someone else do the pre-med.

Rostropovich was a sublime player, if a difficult person. His English was still shaky. The solid thing about him was his wife Galina, who backed him up as a flawless accompanist on the piano. They took the stage at Sanders, the Victorian hall with creaky floorboards and memories of past events encrusted in its mute walls. Here Teddy Roosevelt had spoken, and Churchill, and Martin Luther King. Janos Starker had spooked the hall with an encore of Bach's haunting Sarabande in c minor, a communion with the Dead.

The tension was palpable in the hall. The 200 observers all knew this would be an occasion for the annals – what if Napoleon had met Pushkin? Or Chekhov, Theodore Dreiser? This was the Real Thing, we knew this would be a moment that might somehow survive even the planet.

Two or three fine young cellists had the courage to mount the stage and go through the motions with the Master. Rostropovich was a skilled teacher if condescending. What he couldn't express in English, he demonstrated on his 'cello, dwarfing the technique of those who dared to share a stage with him. Not merely European, but Russian, he was unforgiving of flaws and unmanly tones. In one case he showed how his bow could be imagined as a string of sausages, lurching every eight inches in unsteady progress across the D string. Then he showed how a single bow stroke could remove the sausage links in the sound, and everyone in the room got it. "No sausage, no sausage!" he said, knowing the general laughter would cost the student's self esteem maybe forever, and what of it.

Then it was Yo-Yo's turn. He was not yet histrionic back them – quite the opposite. If I remember correctly back 35 years, he even approached the stage with head bowed. If only we could have him back now, the way he was then.

Slava put his hand condescendingly on Yo-Yo's shoulder and said, "What you are going to play for us this evening?" (He didn't say "young man." He definitely inverted the interrogative.)
In almost a whimper Yo-Yo said "Dvorak 'cello concerto in b minor." Though it was almost inaudible, the crowd went nuts when they understood Yo-Yo was going to take on the signature 'cello piece which—with the Bach *Suites for Unaccompanied 'Cello*—is the measure by which cellists have been judged since 1895.

Slava looked perplexed but fair is fair, so Galina got out the reduced orchestral score and uncrinkled the pages on the piano stand. From the first phrases of Yo-Yo's Dvorak, Slava looked startled, actually disarmed. I think he knew within a couple of minutes that this exotic lad would one day be his rival in the small but conspicuous world of solo cellists.

It was customary to cut off the student after about 15 measures to get to the pedagogical part of the session. In this case he didn't. He let Yo-Yo play almost to the end of the first movement of the concerto. He looked dazed, I can't guess what went through his mind.

The lesson proceeded, Slava brightened up and exceeded even his normal energetic level. His suggestions had to do more with interpretation than technique, which Yo-Yo had clearly nailed. The rest is history, though I've never seen it reported anywhere. At the end of the lesson, Slava embraced Yo-Yo in front of a highly emotional audience and said this time, "Young man, you are a great talent. What was your name, again?" "Yo-Yo Ma," said Yo-Yo, head still bowed. "No," said Slava, struggling with his English. "I mean, your real name."

The audience went nuts as Yo-Yo repeated his name, and the practical joke resolved and was over. We exited into the scented spring night.

At Peace with Nukes?

June 30, 2011

If so, reconsider. Here is Joe Cirincione, President of Ploughshares Fund, flanked by Peter Bergen on his left. June 29 they had a look at doomsday scenarios in a discussion at the New America Foundation. If "Bergen" sounds familiar, it should. His book—*The Longest War*—is the go-to for conflict with al Qaeda.

Have I lost you yet? Nuclear weapons were just a fact of life for the second half of the twentieth century? They kept us scared when we thought they might be used (again), and staying scared kept us relatively safe? Then the Cold War ended, and we looked elsewhere for threats?

I would have skipped the session myself, but something told me I should hear a talk on "Nuclear Weapons in a Changing World."

Nukes, Cirincione said, used to be the core of security 30-40 years ago, and are now misunderstood as peripheral to the core. Rogue nukes are far scarier than accounted ones used to be. Republicans, Democrats, the American public – all seek further reductions in an extravagant nuclear arsenal. "Except in Washington!" he adds ominously.

74

This is not a Grimm's fairy tale; it's the quirk that could do us in.

Let us not misquote Republican presidential candidate Mitt Romney on an issue he has taken to the public—the Ratification of New Start, last year's treaty to reduce redundancy of the nukes we'd counted on both sides.

Here is Mitt's blog from July 6, 2010:

> Whatever the reason for the treaty's failings, it must not be ratified: The security of the United States is at stake. The only responsible course is for the Senate to demand and scrutinize the full diplomatic record underlying the treaty. Then it must insist that any linkage between the treaty and our missile defense system be eliminated. In a world where nuclear weapons are proliferating, America's missile defense shield must not be compromised. As currently drafted, New START is a non-starter.

New START is the New Strategic Arms Reduction Treaty. New START was negotiated to completion in summer of 2010. But when ratification was implausibly stuck in the Senate last winter, five Republican former Secretaries of State spoke on its behalf (Kissinger, Shultz, Baker, Eagleburger, Powell) on December 2, 2010. Robert Gates, George W. Bush's Secretary of Defense who stayed on into the Obama administration, agreed with his five colleagues.
A dead heat between Russia and the United States at best or at worst? And move on? Alas, no: Even if the two countries possess 95 percent of the world's nukes, what counts are the other five per cent!

A scenario need not be likely in order to be terrifying: a nuclear exchange between Pakistan and India could create nuclear winter for the globe. "A loss of two to three degrees would end food production in three years," said Cirincione, "And us."

Now he gets my attention. He's good at this. The Mumbai incident in summer of 2010 might well have been mounted by rogue Pakistani ISI agents seeking to provoke a war between their country and India. They didn't succeed then, but easily could in the future. "Make no mistake," says Cirincione, "A nuclear war in Asia without Europe or North America is still a World War."

We know that sane people would not start a nuclear exchange, and we know equally well that sanity is not a condition for leadership in world affairs. The scenario – now so generally considered that it has its own name – is called "Mumbai II." International treaty structures have kept us intact until now, but just think beyond your teeth, and you see that nations are not the source of the next threat. They are, well, You Know Who.

Ploughshares makes a solid argument: (a) we don't need "parity" in nukes, as just a handful can incinerate us all, and (b) reducing our arsenals gives us the credentials we need to persuade others to do so. In fact, New START has yielded deep benefits in a kind of Russia-U.S. cooperation (read: Iran sanctions) never seen before. Stick and carrot, both approaches lead to the same conclusions and strategy.

Cirincione is a frustrated observer, and you should be, too. The Obama administration made genuine efforts to get the madness under control, but gave up after the Senate *mano a mano* on New START. The administration suffers from "2013itis," says Cirincione. Go the rest of the path now, now, now, or concede to an armament program which will cost $50 billion.

I am not a missile counter, and couldn't pick out a MIRV from an ICBM or SLBM. So don't take my word for it. Look at Ploughshare's website. Or if you want to compare, go to Defense.gov and Global-issues.org.

Add Romney's blog and anyone else's you want.

But this is not just a threat, it's a political imperative, pro or con. And you thought the deficit was a problem!

Looking Back and Fourth

July 5, 2011

I might have posted this last week for the holiday. Can we say I was early for 2012?

A dozen years ago, the July 4 holiday approached at our embassy. It is traditional, but not strictly legal, to enlist Foreign Service Officers to the cause of opening our embassies and houses overseas to foreign publics, for our National Day.

Caryn H. was a junior officer who made more work than she did. Like a gnat in the tropics, she dedicated herself mainly to annoy, with a singleness of purpose you could envy or emulate. Gnats, too, have challenges, anguish, and consummations when possible. "I've found in the Foreign Affairs Manual that federal employees are allowed not to work on federal holidays," Caryn pointed out a week before the celebration.

"Absolutely true!" I said.

"Then I don't have to work at the July 4 celebration," she correctly pointed out. Caryn knew her rights and had done research to prove the point.

"OK, then see you next week when the work resumes," I said. My soul lifted a centimeter to think we would be free of her during the reception. Something like a cloudless sky.

"But I need to know for sure if this is allowed," she said.

My optimism tipped on its side. "I'm saying that it is," I said, ready to move on to my inbox.

"Then I'm allowed to stay home on July 4?"

"Right. I'm your supervisor, and I'm saying that you are," I said.

"I need you to check this out with the deputy chief of mission," she insisted.

I was beginning to lose my lust for life. "I'll call the DCM to make sure," I said.

I called the DCM, who knew her. He said "Great. Let her stay home."

I gave Caryn the good news.

What happened next – if I said, "I couldn't have made it up," I would be saying it not so much to establish the veracity of my story, as to allude to the work ethic now overtaking our nation.

"Then," Caryn said, "Does that mean I'm not invited?"

I repeat: "'Then,' Caryn said, 'Does that mean I'm not invited?'"

I wasn't sure what came next. I needed to get to my work.

"Of course you're invited," I stammered. I wanted to make the machine stop, but couldn't figure out how.

"Find out for sure," she ordered.

I said, "This time you call the DCM. I'm sure you'll be on the invitation list if you want."

Caryn disliked the country where we were, and disliked her work, and our employer. She said we were wasting taxpayers' money organizing low-cost programs for media development. Here is what I might have said to her then, or possibly did say: "If we were friends, I'd like to go into these various issues, and might agree with you on some or up to half of them. Meanwhile before we get to that stage, we should probably do the job we've both voluntarily taken on. While we're in this foxhole we need to do the work.

"This gives you three choices: You can do the work willingly, do it unwillingly, or resign your post. You will be blessed for any of options you choose. I won't think any but the best of you, whichever you pick."

Caryn used to cry when I said things like that. I took out expensive personnel liability insurance, figuring she could sue for psychological damage.

My purpose in telling this story is to assure Caryn, wherever she is, that I'm respectful of her decision to resign her post. I regret only that it took her three more years to decide to do the right thing. Meanwhile she got a plum follow-on assignment, learned a nice language and made the best of it, then quit. She established brave standards of the Individual v. the System.

Caryn had a swain in an exotic country, and requested annual leave pretty often to go be with him. I encouraged her to make those long voyages, because I valued my freedom during her absences, and I loved having her in a good mood for a couple of days after she returned each time. There would be a spring in her step. I understand the suitor was getting frazzled at one point; I guess they have since found the right path for themselves.

I wish Caryn the best. If I ever see her again, I'll thank her for giving me new insights into the meaning of service to ourselves and our country – that is, to one another.

Death Warmed Over in Yaoundé

July 7, 2011

You could be interested to know what a death threat sounds like in a poor country. One of the conventions is the recorded sound of machine gun fire over a cell phone. Clarity and branding are everything.

If you pick up and it gives you "rat-tat-tat," this means either, "Cease and desist," or "I told you so," or "I have the honor to inform you…" With political ambitions, or money in the bank and a school age daughter, you can expect these messages as inevitably as the rising sun.

The problem in one place I know is that, with the power down 90-95 percent of the time, people's cell phones don't get charged. This puts up obstacles for both threatener and threatenee. It can muddle the process and frustrate everyone. Communication can bring horrible things, but everyone wants a message to get where it's going.

So I was in Yaoundé for a month, in a borrowed house a bit too big for one person. You know what this is like late at night. I always liked Yaoundé, though.

80

At 10:20 p.m. the phone went off, and I took the call. A very angry man spoke.

"Espèce de con de connasse d'enculé de merde. On t'aura, tes jours sont comptés." "We know where you are and we'll get you... not if but when..."

I'd received threats before in another country—real ones, face to face from a government official—so this one didn't impress me.

"To whom do I have the honor of speaking?" I asked. This is the way people talk on the phone in Yaoundé.

"You know damn well who I am, and we know where to find you." Click.

The house seemed bigger than it needed to be, by 10:30. I was going to go to sleep, but I realized I should rise to my responsibilities. Three choices: I could go on as if the call had never happened; or report the incident to the regional security officer at the embassy... but I like Yaoundé, and I didn't want to be on the next plane out. The third possibility was to press the "return call" button on the cell phone, on the one-in-a-thousand chance that the caller might pick up.

Amazingly, he did.

"I thought if you are meaning to kill me," I said, "First you might want me to know why."

"Espèce de.." the man sputtered. He explained how his girlfriend had been mugged and her cell phone stolen.

"I sympathize!" I said. "Far too many muggings in this town."
"Blagueur!" the man said. "We can settle this at the police station."

"Glad to," I said, "but which police station?"

There was a silence.

"Is this 94 32 81 70?" he asked.

I checked and said, "It is." You always want to cooperate with someone who says they will kill you.

"And you are the owner of the phone?" I said, "Well, not exactly." The phone belonged to the U.S. embassy, that is, very indirectly to the people of the United States of America.

A longer silence.

"Then I dialed the wrong number," the man said, still furious but now backtracking when he realized I knew *his* number.

"Is there any way I can help?" I said. No need to get indignant at this point.

"Oh just never mind," the man said. And would have said it much more crudely, but people had beliefs in the U.S. government's ability to see them and hear them at all times, and know their thoughts. Something like thinking that rocks and trees have anthropomorphic souls.

We exchanged well wishes, and I went to bed knowing I'd make it through another day.

The point here is not so much that something happened to me, but to see a cross section of the anger and despair out there. Damn thief. To be honest, I hoped the thief would have happen to him what had been threatened to me.

On a tangent, there is also a lesson: life has its real perils, but more often than not, there is a way out. When cornered, just keep moving.

A Summer Read for Our Time

July 8, 2011

Imagine if our current political discourse were free of self deception (the purest form of lie). There are reasons not to lie to ourselves especially, and also to others.

Plausible deniability has a long history, but reached a daring standard with Madame de LaFayette in the seventeenth century. We search with night vision goggles for guide posts through the ambiguities around us. Classics can render them clear and close and beautiful.

The Princess of Clèves (1678) is Europe's first psychological novel, and remains one of the most perfect. You'll find no evil here, nor triumph of ego. Its characters mean well for one another – yet no one gets what s/he wants. Ambivalence? Depends how you define it.

Author Madame de LaFayette's plot, easily parodied, is pretty simple. We are in the court of Henri II, a bit before his death June 30, 1559 in a freak jousting accident. A slightly underage woman, from the family line of Chartres, makes her debut in the Court and dazzles everyone. Going by her best guess and her family's, she marries the Prince of Clèves, an amiable character who isn't a bad catch himself. Only because he comes to adore her does he put up with big doses of anguish. His wife's only wish (her head's, that is, but not her heart's) is to use the Golden Rule with the Prince, her husband.

Cruelly too late to act on it, she sees the one she thinks she really loves — Monsieur de Nemours, a playboy so smitten with her in return, that his libido, well demonstrated in the Court, channels itself solely as devotion to her. Through only hearsay and a Feydeau-like misplaced letter, it is clear they are hooked on each other, but the Prince of Clèves gives wide berth to the Princess.

His willingness to give her total freedom of action on increases her anguish over her errant wishes. She confesses an emotion to him — not a dalliance! — hoping to check a passion and get back to normal. But she refuses to give the name of the object of her affections. The Prince, no fool, figures out on the third try that it's Nemours. We wait for unsheathed swords, but they never come.

Everyone in the triangle just wants to adjust their pantaloons and live up to their expectations of themselves, and of others. Hard to dislike any of them, even if the modern reader might see their sufferings as self-imposed. They are meant for happiness, but contrive ways of denying it to themselves. And all of this, in the imperfect subjunctive!

The excitement of this story is to see the path of conversion from base human impulses into something called civilization. Got to stand up and cheer.

Madame de LaFayette developed plausible deniability to soaring heights. In her many dialogues you will never find a lie, nor will you hear a complete truth. The horrible clash — what people want for themselves versus the volcanic passions that stand in the way — lifts these strong personalities and gets our admiration. Mine, anyway.

This is no chess game. Clèves's knowledge of his wife's attachment to Monsieur de Nemours literally kills him, but his permissive adoration haunts the Princess and shames her into never acting — even with the complete freedom that comes of his death. Nemours's appeal to other women in the Court sweeps the Princess into his orbit, but also causes her to mistrust him. Her discomfort with her husband meanwhile makes a martyr of the latter, and draws her genuine pity and friendship. She feigns illness many times just to get moments of relief, but sticks with her husband even after his death. This is one hell of a mess. And never, ever, does anyone lie – about matters which nowadays would not even get a moment of serious consideration for the truth.

Get this: "'I did not believe,' said Madame de Clèves [to her husband], 'whatever suspicions you might have of Monsieur de Nemours, that you could have any basis for reproaching me for choosing not to see him.'" (translation mine)

Or this: "He found it was greater madness to pass up the chance to come to the place where Madame de Clèves might see him, than actually intending not to be seen by her."

Madame de LaFayette, dust though you are, I love you.

In his last hours of distress, the Prince of Clèves says to his brilliant wife, "You shed copious tears, Madame, for a death of your doing which cannot possibly cause you the pain you exhibit. I am no longer in the position of casting any blame whatever on you... and yet I die of the cruel displeasure you have imposed." Take that.

The Princess, wracked with guilt, defends herself nevertheless ably: "Crimes? Mine?! The very thought is anathema. Only the purest virtue has guided my every act. I have never committed an action I would be ashamed for you to witness." And this is true, to the letter.

During the never-consummated lovers' last words to each other, Nemours says, "You accuse me unjustly, and show me amply how resistant you are to judge in my favor."

She answers, "I admit that passion leads me on; but it will never blind me."

Surrounded with self deception now everywhere, it's time to look back with some urgency, and remember why it is not in our self interest to say a single untrue word, nor the entire truth, either. Living up to it is another matter.

Boom to Bust to Deductible: Hegel Knows Best

July 11, 2011

You can find me at the White House every day this week. Well, not personally, but my ears burn as I become the subject of a big conversation. Supposedly a debate, but it's more like Mozart quartet where each singer stays on his/her motif unwaveringly with a minimum of counterpoint. Counterpoint is what makes music advance "horizontally," and you'll find none of that here.

Shortly after World War II, I was a bump and reached age zero in summer of 1946. Run the math, and you'll see I move into Medicare this summer.

As my classmates and I move from goo-goo to gaga, don't think we don't pick up the unpersonalized resentment of our younger friends who know we might get something out of all this, and they likely won't.

My students are kind enough to keep me out of their rifle sights, but this is only from their nobility and good nature. More from luck than planning, I seem to have enough saved up to keep me in cottage cheese and almonds for the foreseeable future. I wish to heck I could afford a balcony with my condo, but you can't get everything.

This debate we're having: I wish there could be a referee to say, "We've heard your point 30,000 times and we get it. Now proceed to discussion." I won't even say "compromise," as that seems pie-in-the-sky this week.

No one doesn't want Medicare, except I guess all the doctors in America. Less from greed, I think, than from wanting to be doctors rather than accountants.

Now hear this: as the resentful looks dart to me on the Metro (even paranoids have real enemies), I want to say to younger people: "It wasn't my idea. I said, 'Let me pay just my own deductible, and let's be done with it.'"

Let's say one thousand per year. I love deductibles. They keep costs down and catastrophe coverage up.

Wouldn't that bring in a few billion to the Treasury if we all did it? And wouldn't that then give the Democrats the leverage to say, "Now make Buffet spill his pocket change for the Effort. He has said a thousand times he'd be glad to do so"?

Here is the deal I propose: "If I can get five million of us to pledge to pay a deductible on our Medicare, we ask in return that this noise pollution stop and we get back to our geraniums and chamber music." Deal?

The problem is, I know the arguments by heart—we all do—and we crave dialogue and an end to this palaver.

"Not on the backs of the old and infirm." Fair enough.

"Wrong time to raise taxes; it won't work." Well I don't get it, but let's give them the benefit of the doubt. But please make it *stop*.

I know I'm lucky to be able to say, "Make me pay my deductible," but if I weren't so fortunate, I think it would be called "Medicaid" instead of "Medicare."

Very honestly my wish is less for an equitable solution, which there may be, but rather for respite from the noise. To the young, and to my students, I say, "Sure I'll take what I can get, and so will you." But it wasn't my idea for this quartet to slip out of the groove of the LP 78 and repeat… repeat… repeat…

It's an insult to Mozart, who is sublime and who almost always gets from the tonic to the dominant at some point, unless he is changing motifs.

I add a hypothetical question, unrelated to present quandaries: if a nation were to spend a billion dollars every 72 hours on warfare for 120 months, would it affect its disposable income in any way? Just asking.

Smith-Mundt, R.I.P.

July 13, 2011

The death watch has commenced on Smith-Mundt, the 1948 law (P.L. 80-402) establishing a budget and structure for public diplomacy overseas. At a hearing on Capitol Hill this past Tuesday, the U.S. Advisory Commission on Public Diplomacy acted to dismantle a 1985 provision which stated that "No program material prepared in the United States Information Agency shall be distributed within the Unites States" (P.L. 99-93). The Commission will move ahead to table legislation in Congress and have the evolutionary coccyx removed.

One PD-savvy ambassador in the room said, "Get rid of it." No one argued against the excision, and a member of the Commission had to ask three times what possible arguments there might be against it, to get ready just in case.

What was all the fuss about, and what do we lose by canning Smith-Mundt?

Global information is here to stay, and anything going up on the internet is and should be available to all. Before we bury the baby, though, let's look at why it was born: the creation of the U.S. Information Agency (R.I.P. also, as of 1999) was hatched at the end of World War II, proposed as the Bloom Bill (Sol Bloom (D-NY)) in 1945, and later signed as Smith-Mundt by President Harry S. Truman January 27, 1948.

In 1948, the Cold War was well underway, and Congress openly distrusted the State Department to get any accurate information overseas. The State Department was seen in 1948 as "chock full of Reds," a denizen of "loafers," "drones," "incompetents," and "the lousiest outfit in town." (Credit to Commission Executive Director Matt Armstrong for finding these nuggets.) For this reason, and also so as to prevent in perpetuity anything in the United States which might resemble Hitler's Ministry of Propaganda, the firewall went up de facto.

It became de jure in 1985 when Senator Edward Zorinksy (D-NE) said that if USIA ever worked the domestic public, it would be the same as Soviet propaganda (note the substitution of enemies), and instituted P.L. 99-93 forbidding it to do so.

That was before Internet, Twitter, Facebook, and universal information troughs any public can dip into.

Though the law applies only to the Department of State, most funds for overseas information campaigns, though not line items, are allocated to the Department of Defense. Everyone wants the freedom to do their job, so DoD has worked for some five years to get Smith-Mundt removed, in case it should ever affect other Executive departments. There was no threat of extending Smith-Mundt further, though, and State Department Foreign Service Officer Greg Garland blogged March 3, 2009, "Tear down that firewall, and it will be a matter of time before resources and personnel who focus on talking about America overseas are diverted in favor of domestic 'public affairs,' the short-term political imperative of any administration." Any administration savvy enough to understand this tool would do exactly that, and has done so – both Democratic and Republican.

At the hearing July 12, Jeff Trimble, the able administrator of the Broadcasting Board of Governors (a bipartisan group that oversees the Voice of America, Radio Free Europe, and other U.S. government broadcast entities) said convincingly that U.S. government broadcasters would "make no particular effort to disseminate in the United States." Well, that was the point—and the modern meaning—of Smith-Mundt.

One audience member said, "Let's say we trust Jeff Trimble totally, but don't want to give carte blanche to all of his successors!"

Smith-Mundt never forbade U.S. individuals and media from picking up information disseminated by U.S. government entities, it just ruled out domestic dissemination as an end in itself.

Hence you could say, "Why the fuss?" No one has ever gone to jail for "violating" Smith-Mundt, but the principle remains: U.S. White Houses and Defense Secretaries should not use overseas information tools to further their own personal political agendas. Sound good?

Well, it's going, going… gone.

I will not make a big, BIG deal of the passing of Smith-Mundt, as it would identify me as a crank. But Isaac Newton or John Stuart Mill or somebody surely must have said once, for every new liberty, new adjustments to prevent abuse. Not so in this case.

I guess Smith-Mundt will be snuffed out in its sleep sometime in 2012. This note is not a polemic, because clearly the issue has been settled. I only hope to be there for the eulogy, when we honor those who feared domestic dissemination of government information. Imagine, it could be used to sway voters for daring and debatable overseas adventures. And it wouldn't be the first time.

Guinea on My Mind

July 22, 2011

July 19, 3:00 a.m., military fringe groups attacked Guinea-Conakry's newly elected president, Alpha Condé at his residence, but were beaten back after pitched battles lasting to mid-morning. Thirty-seven arrests followed, and a "clean-up" of Guinea's disgruntled and underpaid military.

July 21. In a call-in show on Radio France Internationale (RFI), Guinean expats were roughly equally divided in their conjectures: the assassination attempt was a nicely put down challenge to Guinean's brand new democracy, or was a "montage" staged by Condé himself, to shore up his power.

The world's largest producer of aluminum bauxite ore, and very much a post-conflict zone, Guinea and its recent history are worth a look.

It got to be a country in 1958. That year, calling deGaulle's bluff, Sékou Touré took his country out of the franc zone and staked its future on something called the Guinea franc. Insulted at a speech, deGaulle removed his chips, folded the game, and sent Sékou Touré's Guinea to hell.

Touré led his country to self esteem but turned, himself, into one of post-colonial Africa's first Macbeths. Transforming Guinea into the "Albania of Africa," he made life a hideous punishment for many, and established his own gulag for detention, torture and hangings, with Camp Boiro as the jewel in the crown. Fifty thousand died there, including most of Guinea's educated class. Sékou Touré ended his days in Cleveland in 1984, in the OR as he underwent heart surgery.

Sitting on fabulous mineral wealth and gorgeous countryside, the gloom continued until 2008 with Lansana Conté, Touré's successor – a case of mediocrity turned to senility. Guineans learned that patience was their best virtue and only option.

December 22, 2008, Conté finally died himself. A colorful lunatic, Captain Moussa Dadis Camara, emerged out of a National Council for Democracy and Development (CNDD) and declared himself President. No individual or institution stood in his way.

Dadis said there would be elections, but instead came the "Dadis Show" of *opera buffa* with camouflage fatigues, a television show rivaling Hugo Chavez's in Venezuela: *bravoura*, threats, public humiliations, even the occasional live forced confession of a rival.

When the Guinean people said they'd had enough, and staged a peaceful gathering at the stadium September 28, 2009. Troops fired on them and raped more than a few of the women. So far, nothing out of the ordinary. But then something bizarre happened: the military bickered over who was guilty of the massacre. As Dadis moved to shift blame away from himself, his bodyguard shot him in the head and got away. (Note to self: if my bodyguard ever shoots me in the head, consider a pay cut and sharp reprimand.)

The shooter was no Lee Harvey Oswald, and Dadis was no Kennedy. Moreover, the bullet in Dadis's skull didn't kill him. Observer

George Ayittey said, "Only an empty coconut-head can take a bullet to the head and survive." (No offense to Gabrielle Giffords, who is *not* a coconut-head.)

Though possibly implicated in the stadium massacre himself, the next in line in the CNDD took over. A general, at first subordinated to a captain, became president ad interim. This time when a military leader promised elections, he meant it.

I met General Sékouba Konaté_one Sunday in July, 2010. Loaded weapons and looks of suspicion greeted us on the way in to the presidential palace grounds. A false move could have ruined a perfect day. I don't know if I would have had the nerve to go in myself, but as one of Ambassador Patricia Moller's staff, I knew the president had a weakness for her and saw her as a possible exit from his precarious situation.

We walked past a huge tree and a watering station in the courtyard, with the evening's unsuspecting dinner (a goat) grazing there peacefully.

The president took some time getting downstairs to his receiving room, and looked weary when he did appear. He was on something—pain medication at least—and lumbered under bulky body armor. When you command troops in Guinea, your nights are taken up with anxiety dreams of your own men turning against you.
The president was chivalrous and gentle with Ambassador Moller. The reluctant head of state (many still dispute this) said he just wanted out. The personal and ethnic rivalries in his country daunted him. His own army, the only game in town for young men, was an enormous obstacle to just passing the baton to an elected civilian.

Many suspected him of connivances, embezzlements, plots, and eleventh hour Lucy-and-the-football scenarios of a dashed election. His rhetoric, at least, was consistent: elections within six months and a peaceful transfer of power. Guinea as a nation state, not a brooding confederation of rival clans with daggers drawn.

That Sunday in July, the president made almost no eye contact with us. He was deferential to Ambassador Moller. He liked and respected her. You can skewer your enemies, but never keep a lady waiting if you think she has the ear of the U.S. policy establishment. Guinea was hungry, ready for political maturation and ethnic reconciliation. You could feel it in the air. Everyone gets their chance once, and now it was Guinea's turn.

Konaté's Speech

July 22, 2011

Guinea had its first round of presidential elections June 27, 2010, just within the six month deadline Konaté had given himself. It seemed too good to be true. In all of human history, Guinea had never had a real election.

Two candidates led the pack – ex Prime Minister Celou Dalein Diallo (a Peul) and his rival Alpha Condé (a Malinké, a long time opposition leader, Konaté's Prime Minister, and a resident of France). Civil discourse prevailed, but troubling undertones made everyone edgy.

Of all ethnic groups, Malinké, Forestier, and Sousou had tasted power. Only Peuls had not yet had a chance to rule or misrule their country.

Alpha Condé's speeches were strident, unyielding. Diallo had twice the number of votes in the first round as his opponent, but was not part of the Konaté establishment as Condé was. Time could be on his side, unless Condé could get the second round delayed as much as possible.

The man running the show, General Konaté, fished around for good visas in case anything should go wrong for him in the highly charged atmosphere. U.S. Ambassador Patricia Moller went to bat for him and got him one for the United States, delivered with some pomp August 27, 2010. It wasn't easy, because of Konaté's association with the CNDD, which the U.S. Congress had painted with a broad brush as the guilty party of the stadium massacre of September 28, 2009. While this guilt was well established, the individual degrees of blame were not.

Things heated up in Conakry in 2010, and the date for the second round of elections kept slipping. This worked in Condé's favor. There had been irregularities in the first round, but not enough to affect the outcome. It was, remember, Guinea's first election ever. The election scheduled for July was put off to August, then September...

Konaté went on television August 14, 2010, and delivered one of the great speeches in Africa's history. I am not saying he wrote it, or even that he necessarily believed all of it, though subsequent events indicate that he probably did. Let history note that he pronounced it on national television and put his name to it. The speech was quickly forgotten by international observers but should be resurrected and enshrined:

> [Our young state's] main challenge today is to reestablish an authority so long sidelined and spurned. How do we to do so? By the existence of insubordination, or by flushing it out as a ploy put to the service of special interests.

Konaté then outlined the long trail of disappointments and setbacks to Guinea's advancement on all fronts. This was what Guineans wanted to hear.

> Throughout our tumultuous history, we have suffered under the weight of a state which carried on like a sacred monster, with a horrifying absence of authority to shape its myth.

This is powerful stuff. Then Konaté turned on his predecessor's predecessor, Lansana Conté:

> There was a democratic backsliding and total lack of confidence. The gratuitous extra term of office was carried out in a climate of defiance and distrust, which weakened the Republic and its institutions, and gravely undermined the Guinean social fabric – in particular, a political class overtaken by events and offending through lack of cohesion.

Konaté then sketched the recent history since President Conté's being "recalled by God," with the military as the only element of social organization left in the country. He called the stadium massacre "an act of flagrant defiance, lacking in expertise or legitimacy, the nation's power having discredited itself through bloody repression condemned by the entire world."

This remarkable text then turned to the social division in the country: "The alliance of 'all for one' is as reproachable as a coalition of 'all against one' in going against our social contract and the integrity of our state."

The speech then took a personal note:

> I never claimed to be a superman capable of miracles. I see myself as a man who, among others, dreams of a great destiny for our country: if I can ever be construed as an obstacle, or if I ever harbor a feeling of isolation in my struggle, or if I've lost the confidence of all, I will stop at nothing in proceeding to yet another confrontation against the endless series of misfortunes of my country, and I will step down.

Glasses raised to whoever drafted Konaté's speech that day.

The second round of elections took place November 7, 2010, after five postponements. Alpha Condé and his party, the RPG, took a narrow victory of 4 percent, then went about assuring that Cellou Dalein Diallo and his UDFG kept their political heads down. May

11, 2011, Condé had Diallo's house ransacked, provocation unknown. The Peuls were not happy.

This past week Condé joined all of his successors in drawing fire
from his own military. Most of those arrested were close to the Da-
dis-Konaté intermezzo of 2008-2010. Everyone said the right things
about the incident, and the prevailing interests of democracy: Condé, Konaté, the UN, U.S. and AU, even Diallo.

There is no doubt that Condé benefitted from the dust-up. Maybe,
with Konaté's prep work, and despite the bad behavior of the general's disciples, the "coup" leaders of July 19, Guinea's fledgling
democracy might come out ahead as well. If so, it would mean a lot
to its troubled neighborhood.

Peek-a-Boo

August 3, 2011

Debt crisis? Debt crisis?? The no-tax jackals have prevailed for now, not even their opponents can bear the haranguing any more.

These weeks I'm finding that people duck from my own haranguing on a related subject, and say it is naïve even to try getting back stolen money secured in the world's tax havens. Unfeasible, and in any case, retrieved wealth would likely fall into the wrong hands again anyway.

Really? Not even try?

Coincidence: the amount of wealth hidden in offshore and secrecy jurisdictions is roughly the same as the U.S. debt, adjusted to Tuesday's default aversion in the House and Senate. Gangsters find the tax havens and untraceable accounts easily enough, but so also do MREs (morally repugnant elites) and subtly crafted appendages of corporations, distant but blood relations to the credit and savings institutions we all rely on. No one is untainted.

Offshore accounts have existed since an English prince waited on the island of Jersey in the 1650s to become Charles II. But they never became sophisticated until World War I – when, by the way, the debt ceiling in the United States was created (1917 Second Liberty Bond Act.)

When I say "ten trillion," I refer not just to money stolen from U.S. citizens, but the best estimate of non-resident deposits in secrecy jurisdictions world-wide. IMF estimates are even higher. Is this amount not enough to attract attention? If you think secrecy jurisdictions are a specialty of Switzerland and Grand Cayman, you are woefully behind the times. There are over 60 of them, and they include financial institutions in London, Miami, New York, PRC's Hong Kong, and a host of others.

Like the malaria plasmodium, they adapt faster than the forensics can catch hold of them. The G-20 ("the Greedy Twenty," as they are called in developing countries) have repeatedly called for some restrictions and control of secrecy jurisdictions, but have caved entirely before powerful and skilled lobbies, who have blocked efforts to establish control, including the ill-fated Levin-Coleman-Obama Stop Tax Haven Abuse Act, Senate bill 681, February, 2007. The bill aimed to get back some of the $100 billion lost in the U.S. each year, but never made it to the president's desk.

Yesterday Carl Levin (D-MI) and Chuck Grassley (R-IA) tabled a Bill to Combat U.S. Corporations with Hidden Owners, and an Incorporation Transparency and Law Enforcement Assistance Act. Please pray for these texts to pass.

An Oxfam report says 50 percent of world trade goes through tax havens, and that arresting this would free $280 billion for developing countries (September, 2009). Take that, and the source, for what you will.

It may be my garrulous obstinacy, but I'm noticing that people I talk to about this retreat to resignation and prefer not to know much about it. Too big to fail, too big to fix. But listen up while we all recover from the hangover of the non-default of August 2: we're talking about ten trillion dollars which has disappeared—fwoop—from the world's capital pool.

The two toenail-curling books on this topic are Raymond Baker's *Capitalism's Achilles Heel* and Nicholas Shaxson's *Treasure Islands*. Reading them is as exciting as watching cancer cells grow. But they chronicle terrible destruction.

The top locations of non-resident cash in secrecy jurisdictions are in fact the United States, the UK, and yes, the Caymans – at about 1.3 trillion each. No exclusive finger-wagging, please, at Switzerland, Malaysia, or even at dictators in developing countries who are fleecing their citizens. It's all done by collusion, and we all lose. And continue to do so, until we collectively make it stop.

I found it odd in 2006 when I had to pay Inturist for a hotel in Moscow through a bank transfer to tiny Luxembourg – doesn't Russia have banks? I didn't know at the time that secret accounts in Luxembourg total $2.1 trillion at any given time. Something called the "City of London" (which is not London, but a jurisdiction within the city dating from medieval times) has helped keep UK solvent since the loss of its empire. Soon after the Bretton Woods structure was set up after World War II, it was hastily made into a sophisticated "offshore" entity in the very capital of the country where capitalism was invented.

But the cops and robbers game proceeds only if there are cops roughly pitted against the robbers. In this matter the politics keep the game from even happening: cops are outstaffed, under equipped, and are rendered ciphers in a system where countries are free to compete for capital by offering looser and looser tax havens. The problem is, some individuals benefit, but states and their citizens do not.

If the Doxycylcine is not working and the malaria stays in command, then it's time to get back into the lab and get back to work. It's us versus them.

If the United States alone were able to get back the hidden money just on its own soil, we wouldn't have to hear the tax jackals, because the debt would be manageable. Wouldn't that be reason enough to enable the forensics to do their job?

In Boca di Lobo

August 4, 2011

The world watches as Hosni Mubarak is wheeled in on a gurney to face trial, and Anders Behring Breivik pleads not guilty to acts he acknowledges he committed.

I'm all for defending lawyers doing their work expertly and aggressively, and I'm also for getting the right outcome when it's possible to do so. That's why I'm not a judge – this all just baffles me. Defending reviled figures must be a lonely sort of thing, all the more credit to those who do.

That said—and with compassion to all—is there now a fad to present reviled figures as infirm, insane, or otherwise unable to stand trial? Are the insane responsible for their actions? This is a huge question, and the answer takes wide pendulum swings as societies trade in their paradigms for new ones. This happens once or twice a century, sometimes more.

On July 26, Breivik's lawyer, Geir Lippestad, said to the press, "This whole case indicated that he is insane." We may never know, but possibly Lippestad coached his client to admit to his acts while pleading not guilty, just to reinforce that image. In Norway, a court that agrees to this formula can give a maximum sentence of no more than 21 years, and the prisoner can walk free after 10 years if he/she becomes eligible for parole.

Lippestad faced the press July 26 and spoke freely about his client: "He believes that when you're in a war you can do things without pleading guilty." It is Lippestad's duty to say these things. The surprise is that Norwegian conventions seem to allow him to do so in public, even before the trial.

There is another side to the discussion. Police Security Service Chief Janne Kristiansen, enraged by Lippestad's statements, countered them: "Breivik is evil, not mad."

She spoke to the BBC on camera, the same day: "I have been a defense lawyer before, and in my opinion this is clearly a sane person because he has been too focused for too long and he has been doing things so correctly," she said. "In my experience of having had these sorts of clients before, they are normally quite normal but they are quite twisted in their minds, and this person in addition is total evil."

This is more than a conversation or dispute among jurists awaiting the real skinny from psychiatric experts. It is the essence of a society's take on responsibility for a person's actions. To me it seems that we are in the thirteenth century, if we must turn to sacerdotal pronouncements for guidance on this. The psychiatrist is trained to heal, I think, and to suspend judgment in the process. A psychiatrist would have lots to say about the meeting point of insanity and responsibility—and valuable input at that—but I'm uneasy about a single healer's opinion in a matter that requires a social consensus. It's unfair to the psychiatrist.

Likewise the hair dyed mummy (ok, well, pun intended) on the gurney yesterday in Cairo, behind a cage. The next time I order the killing of two thousand unarmed citizens, I certainly want

Mubarak's lawyer by my side to help me through the defense process. This skilled man has said "the former president is seriously ill," as he may be. The BBC, meanwhile, says, "Our correspondent says many Egyptians are skeptical about this."

Maybe the point is not, "Is he sick?" The point may be, "If he is sick, does he get a pass?"

I repeat: I am not questioning the skill or respect for the professional who defends a reviled figure. We need this as part of the process. I only recoil at the thought of a jury or judge coming down one way or the other, without a guiding social consensus on who is responsible for heinous acts. Lawyers will and should use every trick. Honor and professionalism require it.

The prosecution, meanwhile, is entitled to do the same. I guess Breivik and Mubarak are going to hell, if there is a hell and if there's an afterlife. (That's a lot of ifs.) Meanwhile we should be thinking hard about what to do with the people we'd like to skewer on a hot spike (but we rightfully distrust our instincts) and whether to put them in a cage and throw away the key. There's always frying, if you believe in that sort of thing.

Punitive justice makes the world go round, and some cases go beyond the pale. Meanwhile, if a mass murderer can be separated from his acts either by lunacy or infirmity, so do the rest of us have the right to sequester the actor, as a precaution. And maybe precaution, not retribution or revenge, is reason enough to do so.
Apparently Breivik was planning to get former Prime Minister Gro Harlem Brundland at Utoya, but she was running late that day. I'd love to hear her opinion on ten-years-out-on-parole as a possible outcome.

Getting to YES

August 7, 2011

Here's a bit of tax money you can be glad about, and which yields returns: The Youth Exchange and Study (YES) Program. Created in 2003 by Senators Kennedy and Lugar, YES has been bringing high school students to us from 44 countries. In 2007 the Program began sending American high schoolers to ten countries abroad.

What possible good for our *peau-de-chagrin* shrinking capital pool, you ask? The benefits come long term – you know, the sort of thing the Chinese do very well.

August 4. Our embassy in Accra, Ghana, called in 35 Ghanaian teenagers who had just spent a school year in the various states at high schools, with 35 more at the point of embarking. You can jaw all you want at a Ghanaian about culture shock in the United States, but their peers know better how to explain in context.

Contrast the tentative nature of those about to depart, with the confidence and speaking skills of those just returned, and you see a vivid display of America's future counterparts. All to our benefit, if we intend to go for the long haul.

108

Being discovered, as is our national fantasy, puts us back in a world puzzled at our self- wounding politics and diminishing resources. They "know" we are arrogant, reductionist…until they meet us, and learn of our generally large hearts. This comes mainly through direct contact, and takes most of our visitors by surprise.

Few perceptions match those of a recent visitor, when explaining the phenomenon to peers a year younger:

"You need not fear the family dog, he is well trained and will even respond when you say, 'Down, Rudy.'"

"They have stereotypes, they think we are all track and field stars. I'd never been on a track in my life, but they pressured me to join the team. And guess what, I broke the school record."

"Don't be thinking you can relieve yourself behind the wall of somebody's building, they have this thing called 'Indecent Exposure.'"

"People want to hug you all the time. You must be willing to get used to this."

"A very pretty lady wanted to kiss me. She must have been insulted when I only shook her hand. If I saw her again, I would apologize."

"Don't call your host mother 'Host Mom.' She wants you to call her 'Mom" because she considers you one of the family."

"I was in Vermont. It is cold, so cold. You can't imagine it. Just get outside like the others, and shovel snow."

"They think we always have 95 degrees in Ghana. You must be tolerant of these misunderstandings."

"If they ask you 'Where is your spear,' just say, 'I forgot and left it at home.'"

And most poignantly...

"You must not be shocked by the low academic standards over there. No real work is required as it is here, and everybody gets an A. Just pretend to be challenged."

Indeed, American schools train self confidence well, but with a shrinking basis for the confidence. A Ghanaian teenager catches on quickly, and takes what there is to take.

Observe a deaf Ghanaian 17-year-old saying in sign language, "I cannot adequately thank you," with a sign language-savvy classmate interpreting for the others. No words for the rest of us. This came unexpectedly August 4.

It would be wise to listen closely to these perceptive youngsters embarking on these voyages.

Meanwhile, as our superpower status and credit ratings totter, YES and other exchanges are a smart way of keeping our finger in the global pie while we address the imponderables of our dysfunctions. Here I refer not just to a reduction in conflict (an economically smart move in itself), but also to the long view of our place in a shifting world.

These individual experiences, once gathered, bring to us the partners we will surely need if we are to make it through rough times ahead.

Let Them Show Us

August 12, 2011

This is Charly Ndi Chia, taken from the day I met him in 2005. He was a founding member of *The Post*, a commercially viable daily newspaper in Buea, Cameroon. If there is a braver or more skilled journalist somewhere, I don't know who it would be.

After carpentry, Charly took up journalism at age 17, then joined the news team of the newly created Cameroon Television in the 1980s. Quickly enough, he became director of news, and was the evening anchor of the English edition (Cameroon is officially bilingual).

I don't believe journalists go into the profession intending to prop up deceitful governments. Pressure comes after the fact. At a time of government monopoly on new production and distribution, Charly put up as good a face as his conscience allowed. His signature sign-on—"Live, from Yaoundé!"—became the familiar trademark of the show wherever there were television sets in those early days. But the pressures for "happy news" intensified.

One evening Charly had a P.J. Crowley moment, and cracked under the strain of ever increasing distortions of the truth. "Lies, from Yaoundé!" he started his program, and never regretted it. That historic evening in 1992, he offered a true insight into his real affinities. No one in Cameroon missed the point.

Committing this act of bravado ten years earlier would have gotten him bumped off pretty quickly. As it was, protective friends made it to the station before the police did, and spirited him out the back door. The police got there too late, but probably weren't sure what they would do with him if they'd caught him. It wouldn't have been good. Public shaming of the Cameroonian regime is a dangerous pastime, and people's rage went under the surface but festered and developed over the year.

Charly's curriculum vitae boasts he is "Cameroon's most arrested journalist, with ten detentions." The late Pius Njawe would have disputed this coveted title, as he used to say he'd been arrested over 100 times. But here we get to the fine distinctions between arrests and detentions, and I think Pius was actually detained only once. Charly went to the slammer ten times, which may be the record to beat. The point remains: being a gadfly is a mark of enormous prestige in Cameroon, where journalists regularly used to "disappear" until the Committee to Protect Journalists (New York) and Reporters Without Borders (Paris) put a glaring light on the Biya regime. Knocking off journalists with impunity went out of style, as donor nations began paying attention.

For his *cri de guerre*, Charly takes a notable place in the annals of independent journalism. Maybe an even greater accomplishment was his creation of a profit-making daily, in a country where subsidy and deficit are the only usual options for the printed press. Retreating to his former home along the rainy slopes of the Anglophone Northwest Province, Charly slipped through the clutches and attention of the regime, in a part of the country which generally detests the latter.

Always a man of surprise, Charly married on July 7, 2007. His native town of Buea went nuts, and went en masse to witness the uncharacteristic solemnity. "He cannot be serious," a colleague said. "Charly must be joking." The bride, 40-year-old Rachael Ntube, had had a close medical call that year, but made it through heart surgery in the U.S.

After her abrupt death exactly four years later—also July 7—the priest at the funeral quoted Psalm 83 to a crowd stupefied by the cruelty of it all: "One day within your courts is better than a thousand elsewhere."

A safe guess is that Charly will continue to surprise. Meanwhile, taking on big culprits within his crosshairs, he has secured his honor and that of his profession. Some of the scribes in Western capitals with fancy credentials would do well to emulate him.

Trapezoids

August 28, 2011

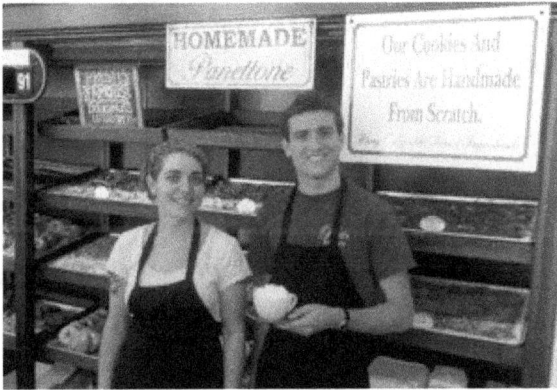

Actually I meant rectangles. You see them everywhere, but almost never in people, plants, lakes, mountains... I would say "nature," but patterns of the human mind are also part of nature. Our bodies fascinate pretty universally, but in the things that please us about them, you won't find any straight lines.

This may seem a leap to comments of my recent rediscovery of Little Italy in Cleveland, but follow me as I try to get us there. I say this with acknowledgement and thanks to the late summer travel sections in the Sunday newspapers, which show me where I no longer need to go, as they went in as someone else's adventure. Plus, the pictures are almost always better than the real thing.

Insular high school students from the "Heights," we seldom made it down Mayfield Road past the cemetery to Little Italy – partly because no one had cars at that age, partly because it was a no-man's-land beyond our parents' comfort. There was disorder there, and coffee, and art in people's flower pots. Implicitly forbidden pleasures, that is.

If one of us borrowed a car on a Friday night we would go down the hill to the vaguely forbidden Mama Santa's. The pizza there was execrable but we loved seeing men cross the tiny restaurant area and disappear into the back room, not to reemerge. Something was going on. This last phrase has an ominous tone, but also had delights for those of us with an overdose of order. We feared the misdemeanors we hoped were taking place, and imagined police and random bullets. But you don't climb to the rim of a volcano just to do a volte-face without casting a glance first at the cauldron below.

Little Italy had been built of rectangles decades before, but never abided by them fully. There should be a reason why it became "Little Italy" instead of "Little Prague" or "Little Beijing," but we imagined its origins as contemporaneous with the arrival of Aeneas from Carthage to the Italian peninsula.

I am playing on our innocence here. We were lured by the East, the East (Pittsburgh, New York, the Levant…) and oblivious to a treasure in our midst.

Late summer is the time Little Italy was meant for, and I went to have a look last week, while in town for a visit. Some *trattorias* were closed for the season, but *flâneurs* stepped into Presti's for cappuccino and pastry. Mothers and fathers guiding their toddlers, impossibly good looking young people, jovial brutes taking an afternoon break and sitting by the street side patio facing Murray Hill Road. Other places had maitres d' deployed on the sidewalk, but no hard sell, no recruiting. No opulence either, but little refuges like Bacio and Nido and Patrizio's.

The dark vestiges of earlier fear and fascination were lifted as if on a color emulsion, maybe also removed by the passage of decades. What was once exotic (in many places in general, I mean) can become familiar, almost commonplace.

In the 1950s and '60s, looking good was seen as a self indulgence, a narcissism, and now is a forest of riches. Things progressed without us and beyond us, and it's a good thing they did.

The same sort of sun and floral displays you would find along the Mediterranean, since became exposed and known to all through pictures, moving and otherwise. Anyone got to see them up until the Spanish Steps in Rome withered under the broken beer bottles in recent years.

Frontiers remain, many fed by memory and new glances at old familiarities.

I am not advocating yet another unendurable plane flight to nowhere. I only note that these worn streets now open to me and anyone who cares to venture there. This is more about me than it. But if in ordinary Cleveland old bottles can bear new wine, then discovery (the main reason for living) is there for anyone who can cleave unto it in unexpected offerings.

Again to the Breach

September 18, 2011

Ohimè, Cameroon looks at elections again, October 9. The Executive has the voters where they want them, divided and incapacitated. With over 30 candidates for president, the incumbent, Paul Biya, is a shoe-in for a fourth term of seven years. Only Muammar Ghaddafi exceeded him in years in office for a head of state and chief of government, well, until earlier this month.

Already in his third term, Biya arranged for a constitutional amendment in 2008, removing term limits for the president, even as the Nigerian parliament blocked a similar effort the same year. He has led his country since 1982. The only heads of state outlasting him are Hassanal Bokkiah, Sultan of Brunei (1967), and the monarchs of England (Elizabeth II, 1951), Sweden (Carl XVI Gustaf, 1973), and Spain (Juan Carlos, 1975). But these latter three were not heads of government. Recent rivals in longevity were Muammar Ghaddafi (1969), Yemen's Ali Abdullah Saleh (1978), Egypt's Hosni Mubarak (1981), and Tunisia's Zine el Abidine Ben Ali (1987).

September 13, a delegation from Cameroon's government presented a bright outlook for the October 9 elections at the Wilson Center, in Washington, DC. Cameroonian Ambassador to the U.S. Atangana Joseph, Cameroonian Electoral Commission (ELECAM) President Fonkam Samuel Azu'u, PM Senior Advisor Fabien Nkot, and Director of Cabinet Ghogomu Paul Mingo, gave detailed plans indicating an open and transparent process. Freedom of the press abounds, minus the occasional prison homicide (Germain Ngota, *Cameroon Express*, killed during detention April 22, 2010) and the skillful patronage which keeps perennial opposition leader John Fru Ndi and others at modest levels of electoral support. John Fru Ndi is the Norman Thomas of Cameroon, except for his very friendly relations with the current head of state.

The only glitch in the proceedings September 13 was the open rage of the Cameroonian diaspora in the audience. One questioner asked "How can you sleep at night, supporting a president who has done nothing for his country in 29 years?" Another, "We challenge the validity of candidate number four [Paul Biya], given that his steam-rolled amendment of 2008 is not retroactive, and therefore disqualifies him for a fourth term under the previous Constitution."

Fabien Nkot responded, "We are not perfect, but we are improving."

The presenters have learned well the language of comfortable heads of state, and welcomed the dialogue, championing free speech. They noted an economic growth rate of three per cent in 2010, and affirmed that President Biya's goals of his second seven-year mandate have been realized. This might come as a surprise to the average Cameroonian, but the data supports the assertion. In the country ranked number one for corruption in the world during four consecutive years in the 1990s by Transparency International (with corruption costing Cameroon some $3.75 billion from 1998 to 2004 according to Agence France-Presse), the panel assured that "the government is waging a relentless war against corruption."

Politics and elections in Cameroon are not genteel. In 1992, political protests were brutally crushed, and in 2008, food price rises resulted in a presidentially ordered massacre of 150 peaceful demonstrators across the country.

Cameroonians are not stupid, and have their code words for despair: "In Cameroon, everything is possible," is the well known phrase meaning, "With a bribe, here you can get anything. The variant is, "In Cameroon, nothing is impossible."

Then there is "The Cameroon of Great Ambitions," a phrase offered by the Head of State which turned against itself and is now a term of derision.

When challenged by Woodrow Wilson host Steve McDonald on a police attack on radio station Magic FM in 2008, the panel was well equipped with answers, but did not explain the destruction of VOA equipment during the attack. They pointed out that "administrative tolerance" allowed broadcasters free rein, but omitted to mention the sliding scale of license fees would cost most broadcasters four times their yearly income – and the notions of co-opting and intimidation come to mind.

Asked about the economic future of their country, the panel confidently responded, "We have a plan." This did not satisfy the diaspora audience.

At 78, Paul Biya's health issues keep him in Switzerland and France some 60 percent of his time, and necessitated a one-million-dollar stay in a luxury hotel in southern France in summer of 2009. His occasional arrival in his own country is generally front-page news. The International Crisis Group characterizes the situation in Cameroon as a "slow burn crisis" of expectations. We look forward to the election opportunity in three weeks time, for improvement in this area.

The good news, in the words of a high ranking Cameroonian official in 2009, is that "Cameroon may not be heaven, but it is not hell either." That official is now in jail in Yaoundé, where he belongs. This gives us hope for a break in Cameroonian electorate's chronic apathy and rage, when they consider the wealth stolen from them and residing in secret, numbered bank accounts in Switzerland, Luxembourg, Malaysia, and—yes—the United States.

Cameroon can always surprise, and it could yet do so October 9. I hope it does.

Another Chance for DRC

September 21, 2011

This is Salima Etoka, "from Idaho," but it's a bit more complicated than that.

Born in Bukavu, Democratic Republic of Congo, she escaped genocide and rape as an infant, in one of the most beautiful landscapes on the planet.

Her parents knew someone who knew someone, so they traveled to Burundi for respite from the destruction of communities in eastern Congo, in the most violent and sustained human bloodletting since World War II. They fled to Cameroon, but were held in detention there for two months when it seemed they lacked the proper documents to enter the country.

They retreated to Kenya around 2000, then stayed in a holding pattern for two months more before reentering Cameroon, this time successfully.

With the help of a family sponsor in California they received a DV (diversity visa) and were set to emigrate to the United States. The attacks of 9/11 delayed the DV process, but they did fly to California late in 2001.

"The people of California were not hospitable," Salima says with a forgiving smile. "So on a tip we moved to Idaho, where there was room for us."

Salima is now registered at Trinity College, in Hartford, Connecticut. She speaks native-level English, plus French and Swahili. She is interested in the history of race relations in America, but also foreign affairs, economics, and peace and conflict resolution. Her approach to her past and future is bright and benign. She talks to her grandparents back in Bukavu every week, from her cell phone to the one they rent or borrow for the weekly call. This week they were still alive.

Salima understands that as one of the few to escape the killing fields of her native DRC, her good fortune comes with ethical and moral obligations to reenter her world armed with savvy and a methodology to staunch its wounds.

The methodology will come, the exact application to be revealed. Salima has considerable weight of memory and responsibility on her young shoulders. She finds humor in her unlikely circumstances.

Meet her here, she is the future and a possible breach in the Maginot Line between the fortunate West and the betrayed others left behind. Few will find the breach in that Line, but with another lucky break or two, Salima will do so.

While They Slept

September 23, 2011

Nicholas Cull is USC's prolific scholar and author on Public Diplomacy in the United States. September 19 he talked to a group of retired PD officers, on "Understanding the Decline, Death, and Afterlife of USIA."

The U.S. Information Agency was swapped by the Clinton administration in the 1990s for a vote on a chemical weapons treaty. Tactics and strategy came head to head in this barter with Jesse Helms (R-NC). Tactically successful, the swap left USIA survivors unimpressed.

Nick Cull knows how to please a crowd, and engaged in grief therapy with an audience still stunned by an agency's demise twelve years earlier. "I mourn the disconnect from what you were doing," he said, "and the absence in the White House of your insights at the highest level of policy making."

Cull pulled no punches, indicting U.S. policy makers over two decades of "privatitis" (the belief that the private sector can conduct foreign policy), of "isolationism," "arrogance," and "anti-professionalism." Imagine an audience in one room with a collective memory of 1,500 years, being told by an expert that their experience was valuable and even irreplaceable. Even the rubber chicken went down well for the occasion.

Looking back to look forward—*reculer pour mieux sauter*—Cull noted that U.S. triumphalism of the 1990s after the end of the Cold War was a squandered opportunity, and that U.S. efforts to project its soft power at that time should have been augmented, not dismantled.

Many in PD today would argue that the Public Diplomacy function of the U.S. government was not dismantled at all, only reorganized and redeployed. Strictly speaking they are right to say so.

Still, the Cull talk reminded me of the panel discussion I joined in 1994 when USIA still existed. A dozen of us spent five months and 50 hours pondering the future of an office called Arts America, which sent out performers, artists, consultants, exhibitions, and samples of U.S. artistic endeavor. Dance troupe Pilobolus and violinist Mark O'Connor got their start in this way, as did a number of others. I took O'Connor myself, to Egypt, Jordan, and Syria.

Little did we know, during those five months sequestered, that the decision to eliminate Arts America—entirely—had already been made.

Cull cited USIA director Joe Duffey and his deputy, the late Penn Kemble, as telling him in the mid 1990s that their mission was to show "the Cold War was over."

"Craziness," said Cull, and cited an English folk expression: "The dog is not only for Christmas." One lives through one's good and bad fortune, enduring. It used to be said that Americans seek to solve their problems, the French debate theirs, the English outlive theirs. This was in a narrow Western context, and has more applications now as other cultures show us the value and triumph of

124

strategy over tactics – the long haul. China understands this, and oversees a proliferation of Confucius Centers to share its culture ("soft power") in other countries, while our own equivalents cede to security and budget exigencies.

Poor Kemble, by the way. I hate to kick the deceased, but if his CIVITAS conferences (at $500,000 a pop) were a mark of his ego and legacy, then we all wondered why he failed to attend the one we conducted in Pretoria in 1996. I wish I could ask him now, what matter was so important as to prevent his attending and observing its success.

Soft power, then. I had a chance to meet Joseph Nye September 8 when he spoke at American University. I asked him if he was bothered by the universal and persistent misuse of his terms "soft," "smart," and "hard" power in political discussions today ("smart" cited when "soft" is meant.) Nye invented only the terms, not the actions.

He laughed benignly and said to me, "Oh, I understand no American politician can use the word 'soft.' It would seem weak. Moreover, smart power is big enough to encompass soft when it has to." A charming and forgiving touch on his part. Before PD is further diminished in the next budget, however, policy makers and Congress will have to agree whether we have anything left to say to other countries, or any systematic listening we might want to conduct, as the captains of industry learn to capture cow farts and channel the energy needed for a future industrial renaissance.

Both efforts will require some humor, humility, and a dose of shame for opportunities lost.

Tactics will often "triumph" over strategy, but the long haul is the one that matters, and we have some 'splaining to do, and some methodical listening as well.

Sandy and Henri

September 24, 2011

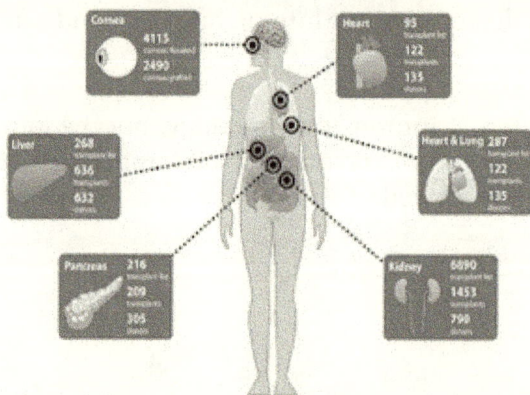

Sandy was a taxi driver and sitar player in New York, then later worked with me in the Bureau of European Affairs at the State Department. He said he picked up his hepatitis at a dentist's office in London.

Henri was a photographer for *Der Spiegel*, working out of Jerusalem. He was the husband of a good friend.

Both needed livers. Donated organs are hard to come by, and then there is the question of organ rejection even when blood types are compatible. Even half a liver helps, as livers grow inside the rib cage as long as they can get a fair start.

Both friends seemed at the edge in 2002, each was on a separate waiting list for organs that might come available. Most on these lists die while waiting.

Sandy looked terminal. I flew to western Massachusetts a couple of times, either to encourage him or say goodbye.

Henri waited with his family in Philadelphia, I drove there from DC a few times for the same reason. They never knew each other, there wasn't time for that. Luckily they never "competed," as the lists are made up geographically, and Philadelphia and New England go on different systems.

Of the two, Henri retained his joie de vivre. You could tell he was very ill, but he joked throughout. Sandy had a great sense of humor, but his pain obscured it.

Months passed, and both cases became dire.

Amazingly the two received organs from the separate lists at about the same time. Sandy called me from the recovery room describing his euphoria. He was goofy with delight, and seemed to be discovering life with new appreciation.

Henri received his as well in the eleventh hour, but did not make it out of surgery. His wife and children took the many mourners to dinner after the memorial service a month later.

Sandy lives fully, back in western Mass. Henri is gone. We seek meaning when these things happen. I say there is none, but I accept the arguments of others who say "there must be."

But lessons, yes. We learn three lessons from this brief story:

1. Honor your friends while you can.
2. Miracles happen, but not always.
3. Donate your organs, you won't miss them the day they are needed.

Jacques Among the Living

September 27, 2011

If Jacques Jost were to rise from his grave today and hear someone say to him, "You filthy slob," he would probably take it as flattery. He was our French professor at Boston University in the 1970s. He liked the fermented grape, the stench of cigarettes, his native language, and something they call *désinvolture* – flippancy. He hated pretense but loved Molière, the patriarch of nailing and unmasking hypocrisy.

Jacques marveled only at the French Revolution, which he saw as step one of bringing down unearned privilege. He respected nothing except maybe the tricolor, the revolutionary banner which still stands as the flag of France. Though he did so mockingly, sometimes he would stand at his version of attention at the very mention of it.

His colleagues despised him, and he them. I think he liked or loved his students, whose names he never bothered to learn. We must have seemed unspoiled to him. For three decades he shared close quarters in a tiny office with a colleague. The two never exchanged a word, not even in the morning. Everyone knew they hated each other.

Friday afternoons Juan the Spaniard and I would join Jacques in the Dugout, a dingy bar on Commonwealth Avenue, which still exists. Through clouds of cigarette smoke Jacques would tell filthy jokes and French slang for topics like undertakers, gynecologists, urologists, and the police. He loved the power of his language to create and dismantle puffery, using words from the same vocabulary for opposite purposes. French has one third the number of words as English. It has a way of biting its own tail, as when in melodious tones it says *"le boulevard des alongés,"* which is, well, a cemetery.

Jacques had no known life, and kept to himself. He was blind to charm and had none of his own. A ball of saliva would often form on his lower lip as he talked to us conspiratorially, and he had trouble catching his breath. He wore an ancient leather jacket which could never have been cleaned. He got angry sometimes but usually blandly dismissed the things and people who crossed him. He didn't seem to mind being ugly.

Complete candor was the only attitude he knew, and with it came the stuff of offense. Either you put up with it to get the jokes and slang, or not. I didn't much like the Dugout, but I liked my Friday afternoons with Jacques and Juan.

One day the inevitable happened, and Jacques didn't show up for the weekly staff meeting. Someone had to go find out where and how he was, but no one had any idea how to reach him. Research through the files showed he had no phone, but did live in a flat on Beacon Street. The prof he most despised, and shared an office with—but never words—was assigned to go out and track him down. When he did so that same day, he found Jacques dead in his tiny one-bedroom.

The cause of death was something like life, or having used up what there was of it. We don't know if the one who found him dead on the floor ever had remorse for shunning him for 30 years.

It couldn't have been pleasant to find him like that. Jacques was shoveled away somewhere. People were sort of relieved to be rid of him, but I was sad to lose him.

We learned that Jacques had sired a daughter at some point in New York, and as next of kin she was informed of the death. We never found out if she had any opinion of him.

A couple of weeks later the university organized a memorial service, in its chapel now named after Martin Luther King. Some knuckle brain put an organist to work playing a solemn repertoire, the sort of thing Jacques most disdained.

An empty coffin lay symbolically at the altar. To the astonishment of all, the chapel quickly filled to capacity with a couple hundred stray individuals—past and present disciples—none of whom knew any of the others. In the same way that Jacques had spent his Friday afternoons with Juan and me that year, it seemed that others had had their turn in years before. They all came to spend a moment remembering him. No one knew Jacques had touched so many people.

Then the laughter started, somewhere around the middle of the chapel. Everyone had the same thought simultaneously: if Jacques had really been in that coffin, he would have heaved himself out of it and said, "Let's get the fuck out of here and have a beer at the Dugout."

I slipped out the back of the chapel to go across the Avenue to the Dugout for a last drink there, but dozens of others had had the same idea, and the splintery bar became packed as well. Verifying that we'd all had the same image of Jacques rising out of the coffin to mock the solemnity of it all, we laughed yet harder, as Jacques might have wanted. Later we exited into the spring grime of the Avenue, and went to whatever was next.

Spending those Friday afternoons with him pretty much rooted out respect or tolerance for blather. I probably produce blather myself, but I have a low threshold to hear or see it. Unwittingly he left his mark with many, something he would never have done by design. The constellations, whose anthropomorphic meanings Jacques would scoff at, likely embrace him now. He considered deconstructionism a crock, but his life was a good rendering of the stripping away of artifice. Molière's was the only structure he accepted. He would be disgusted to know of any effort to find or imagine his current locale.

He taught unexpected numbers of us that we need not believe much, that in youth there is some virtue, and that pretense and presumption are very grave crimes. Pace, Jacques.

At It Again

October 19, 2011

Tip of the hat to Michael Gerson, for his op/ed of October 18 on those pleading a case for Joseph Kony, Lord of dismemberment of humans in Uganda, Central African Republic, Congo, and Southern Sudan. This most vile individual has found unwitting allies in Michele Bachmann and Rush Limbaugh, little did we know.

As I dropped out some time ago from listening to these two, but for Gerson I would never have noticed they had opinions on Kony. I suppose we should note these disparagements—or take turns doing so—to see how far ignorance has taken us.

You like random hackings of the limbs of the uninvolved? Gang rapes of eight-year-old girls (and boys)? Slavery put to the purpose of terrorizing defenseless villagers away from the view of the Western public eye? Cruelty with no ideology or objective? Then you'll love Kony and his Lord's Resistance Army. Evidently the word "Lord" snookered the guardians of American morality into supporting or tolerating them.

Not that I can improve on Gerson's piece connecting the dots. The only embellishment to add is that, in contrition, I link my own ignorance to that of Bachmann and Limbaugh and friends, as a factor in our flirtation with a state of being derived from ignorance, and its companion, sadism without a purpose.

The French put it well: "Intellectuals should not be allowed to play with matches." The only issue with this bit of Gallic folklore is its use of the passive voice, suggesting the presence of an adult to prevent them from doing so. In this case there isn't one, just our cherished freedom of speech. Here we have *Lord of the Flies* without the rescue scene at the end.

If the public knew the context of these assertions, they would not stand for it. After all, we are softened by a sweet morality infused at times with pity and compassion. (Cinema and literature have figured heavily here.) And yet we sin by inaction, in repelling the information around us, like infants spitting out their formula. This we all do, every day.

The enemy of course is not people, but ignorance. Wait a minute, though: the individual who is guilty of ignorance gets forgiveness only on the condition of keeping his/her mouth shut. The sin and the sinner are separable, but if the sinner repeatedly selects sin, s/he should meet stiffened resistance from the rest of us – lacking which, shame on us.

I am not trying to objectify or vilify Bachmann or Limbaugh – they too are people (I guess) with heads and hearts and foibles. If only they would keep the microphone in the "off" position, we would all benefit.

My penchant is with the victims. The perpetrators (that is, those who profane humans in public) can construct their own hell as well, since we others are not equipped to do so. The sooner they reach their destination, the better for all.

The Third Commandment forbids taking the name of the Lord in vain. You can have some issues with the Commandments in general, but those who take them unquestioningly should be nailed when they violate them. An apology from these two would be a good start in the right direction. I do not believe they are really degenerates. Because of my cheerful optimism about humans, I wish they would say something to prove it.

Sarith's Story

October 31, 2011

Sarith Sok was born more or less in 1953 in Kandal Province, Cambodia, near the border with what was then South Vietnam. A year later, defeated at Dien Bien Phu, French forces left the region they called Indochina, and bestowed independence to Cambodia, Laos, and Vietnam.

Pierre Mendes-France, France's 143rd prime minister, advised the United States to avoid the ongoing conflict. Americans at the time were in awe of French baguettes and cheese, but not their policy advice.

At the age of eight, after his father's death, Sarith was moved to Phnom Penh, and entered third grade. North Vietnamese recruiters trolled for young Cambodians to join their forces and gave the pitch to Sarith, who found their invitations intriguing. His mother said no. Others were kidnapped and programmed to join the North Vietnamese cause.

In 1970, Pol Pot commenced civil war in Cambodia with the co-operation of Prince Sihanouk, while General Lon Nol fought off the North Vietnamese to retain a modicum of independence for his Cambodia. Sihanouk, meanwhile, opened the border to allow North Vietnamese into Cambodia to provide a staging platform for the North's war against the South. It was all a trade-off.

Also in 1970, Richard Nixon ordered "secret" bombardments of North Vietnamese supply lines in Cambodia, which the North used to attack the South. Sihanouk denounced the action as a violation of Cambodia's neutrality.

The Cambodian civil war, 1970-75, gave the Khmer Rouge primacy in the country, and led to the genocidal killing of one-fifth of Cambodia's population.

Sarith Sok was moved by Pol Pot forces to an area near the Vietnamese border, and worked a farm in 1978-79. Toward the end of the civil war period, Sarith walked 500 kilometers from the north of Cambodia to find his family back in Kandal province, then under Vietnamese occupation. He reached his destination and did the inventory of his relatives, alive and dead. He decided to go west, to Thailand, and escape the whole, sorry mess.

In 1981 Sok traveled by foot, train, and motorcycle to the Thai border, there encountering five obstacles to survival: Vietnamese troops still occupying the western parts of Cambodia, land mines, Cambodians still fighting Pol Pot forces near the border, highway robbers, and Thai soldiers tasked with keeping Cambodian refugees out of Thailand by shooting at the ones trying to get in. He was advised by friendly Cambodians at the border not to try to cross the border by day.

Sok waited in the night to receive coded messages by lamp from Cambodian refugees in the Kaoi Dang refugee camp in Thailand. One night at 2:00am he saw the green signal, and made his break for the camp, arriving by foot.

After two years in Kaoi Dang camp he was allowed to try his luck at Western embassies in Bangkok, to get out entirely. The Americans refused his visa request, noting that he had no proof of fighting sufficiently against communist authorities in Cambodia when he could have done so.

The Canadians saw his case differently, and stamped a visa in his Cambodian passport, telling him he must move to Canada within 30 days.

In 1983 Sarith Sok arrived in Toronto, where he was given a temporary room in the Waldorf Astoria, and given five Canadian dollars for other expenses. After he married a Cambodian domiciled in Lancaster, Pennsylvania, in 1985, he later moved to Pennsylvania "Dutch" country in 1987 and in 1990 produced a daughter, Monica. Now a senior at American University, Monica took a Boren scholarship in 2010-11 to study in Vietnam, and learn the languages of Vietnam and her ancestral Cambodia. She would have gone to Cambodia, but the Hunsen Sen regime currently in power there does not provide a stable academic environment for study.

Sarith says I am his "brother," which suits me fine. This would make Monica my "niece," which gives a nomenclature for our strong friendship.

Sarith visits me in Washington every couple of months, and brings Caesar salads and salted almonds from Pennsylvania. I have received far more from him than I ever might have provided. Such are the imponderables of unlikely friendships.

Draft bait in the 1970s, I declined the honor of serving with U.S. forces in Southeast Asia. I had mixed feelings about the stand I took then, and I still do. Sarith says that Richard Nixon's "violation" of Cambodian neutrality in 1970 was the only decent thing to do, and I learn this only 40 years later. It is one man's opinion.

The ambiguities of power, violence, assistance, aide to the underdog, "responsibility to protect" ("R2P") seem never to release their claws' grip holding back clear truths.

Sometimes friendship is the one thing left, a rare remaining value in a world where cruelty and idiocy still prevail.

My Southeast Asia

November 2, 2011

I've never been there, but the U.S. government sought my assistance in neutralizing communism there in 1968, '69, '70, '71, and
'72. I declined the honor – not from fondness for communism, but
from seeing in news reports that a lot of Asians and Americans
were being killed in the conflict, and I didn't see the cause of human freedom or dignity or survival advanced by getting a lot of
people killed.

Thirty-five years later in Boston, I was on a panel judging applicants
for the U.S. Foreign Service. A young Vietnamese man was brought
before me for consideration. He was born in Boston, of Vietnamese
immigrants. Luckily my colleague Harriet was in the room at the
time, as I lost objectivity when I glanced down at the candidate's
birth date. I noticed that the year of his birth was the same as the
one when I had been called to service to eliminate wrong-thinking
Vietnamese in the interest of free markets and freedoms of movement, expression, and integration into the civil society.

This young man is in the room with us today, I thought, because I did not kill his father.

Well, many legions of U.S. troops did not kill the father, also. However, to be one of the many gave me pause. It is enormously likely I would not have killed the young man's father, and yet I could have. I was stymied in the process and turned to Harriet to conduct the interview.

Ethical questions arise. Students tell me now that they meet men of my generation, who ask for favorable consideration for their acts of the 1970s, and pointing out they were not asked their opinions before being deployed to Southeast Asia to join the combat against an oppressive communist system. Many went. Fifty thousand were killed in the effort. In truth I don't miss the dead, as I never knew them.

The survivors now ask for "forgiveness" of students two generations younger. A profligacy, I would say. Those asking for forgiveness had other options, and chose not to take them. The information they needed to make fully informed decisions was readily available, even to saturation.

Those asking for acquittal do not state their offenses. They killed how many, before seeing that their actions were tainted? They do not say.

Nor do they direct their appeals to the victims, who are not available to provide forgiveness, as they happen to be dead.
These are serious matters. The sympathetic recanters ask for pardon for acts done against those now gone. The rational answer would be, "Find the victim first, and ask that one instead."

Forgiveness comes cheaply these days, and is handed out by those not qualified to give it. Most annoying, those who plow into the masses of the uninvolved, seeking what cannot be given. Short of a phony thumbs up, one can always say, "You did as you had to, now proceed."

140

It is not for me to decide, but I think forgiveness is the exclusive realm of the victim. If the victim happens to be dead, seek the life you can, but do not ask others for a judgment that is not theirs to offer. For the *génocidaires* we say, we grant you the death you dealt, ask for no more.

Imploring innocents for "forgiveness" for acts they know not is moral blackmail. I hope today's young will take the Fifth, and leave the *génocidaires* of the 1970s to deal with their own demons. I do not condemn them for the deeds, only for their groveling to those unqualified to redeem them. Let crimes lie with neither retribution nor release. The young may pursue and construct their own demons, they need not inherit those of their antecedents.

Blaming No One

November 13, 2011

Everyone has Kafka experiences. We should thank Franz for setting the standard and lending his name to the effort of finding patterns in them. Any one of them is as good as the next. Like incantations, they can lead to a healing process in the very telling of them.

People who impose or exercise the Kafkaesque scenarios we all endure are mainly blameless, but leave us wondering how the human brain halted at a certain point in its development. Brain-body proportional relationships in humans are favorable for the brain and related attributes like compassion, ethics, morality, and finding the way out of a maze. We're told that the fight-flight mechanisms evolved for an earlier age, so the mismatch of our functions to our tasks usually comes out as comical. Frustration is, itself, comical from the moment we observe, rather than endure it.

I seek relief in telling my recent story.

November 10. I took students to the Dirksen Senate Office Building for a public hearing on Syria policy. The hearing was lush in its descriptive power and universal disgust for Bashar al-Assad's excesses and violence against his own people.

As I wouldn't want to be a member of a club that would admit me, I honor security checks and value the diligence of those who conduct them. November 10, I put my cell phone, keys, and change in the little dish that goes through the X-ray machine, then had the uneasy moment, during the seconds when the dish emerges to the safe side of the check before we do.

The fateful day this finally did happen, as I found my cell phone and change in the X-ray dish, but saw that my key ring was gone – poof. No one's fault, it just happened. I never actually saw the dish come out of its machine before I came out through mine, so I suppose the keys either got into someone else's pocket by inadvertence, or stuck to the roof of the X-ray machine like peanut butter. Maybe they were vaporized and reconstituted in another space-time continuum.

The security guards at the Dirksen were sympathetic, but weren't able to locate my keys after a pretty lengthy search. I imagined myself without a house or car, realizing that misfortune happens, and people overcome it almost all the time.

Two hours later, after the Senate hearing, I went back to the security guards who helpfully directed me to the Dirksen building's lost-and-found, where I was shown a large box with 30-40 lost key sets. The lost-and-found people displayed their key sets with some pride, like merchants at a souk, and elegantly offered to me any one I might want to take. None of the sets matched mine, though.

The next day I googled the Dirksen Building, and saw lots of information on the site but no phone number. I dialed 411 and knew the quest would not be easy when the operator asked me to spell "Senate," as in, "What sort of business is it?"

The operator connected me to Senator Cochran's office, where I tried to maintain congeniality in asking for the Dirksen main number.

"I'll connect you," the Cochran employee said helpfully.

"Many thanks," I said, hoping for the main switchboard number. But it wasn't. I was transferred to a non-working U.S. government number with a dead-end recording. I called the Cochran office again and tried to be cheerful. "We spoke a moment ago, I hope you'll accept my thanks for your help. Could we try the security office of the Dirksen Building?"

"I'll connect you," said the Cochran office, and did so before I could ask for the phone number of the Dirksen security office. The call went through to the Capitol Police.

"Which building?" asked the Capitol Police operator. This seemed like progress.

"I'll connect you." I asked for the number for future reference, but the operator only connected me back to the Cochran office.

"Hi there, it's me again," I said.

In the end, the effort didn't succeed, and despite everyone's good will those keys are somewhere in a reconstituted molecular structure in an unknown location.

I'm inclined to think I deserve the punishment received in this looped experience. I will gladly cooperate, cop a plea, do what is required, but I would so long to know what my offense was. I would plead guilty if only I could know what the charges were.
But I aim high here. And the meaning of Kafka is that punishment may never fit the crime, or any crime at all. It's funny, even to me, but I don't know why. Someone should figure this out as our opportunities for frustration spread like an opening desert flower at dusk.

Bad Boy Gbagbo

December 13, 2011

Laurent Gbagbo, former president of Côte d'Ivoire, was arraigned by the International Criminal Court November 29 for alleged crimes against his own people.

He is the first former head of state to face this predicament since 2002. The ICC wants Omar Bashir of Sudan (recently even Kenya said it would extradite him to The Hague if they got their hands on him) and Muammar Ghaddafi, but the latter was plugged by his own Libyans before the ICC got its chance.

ICC prosecutor Luis Moreno-Ocampo made it clear that the Court holds Gbagbo accountable for acts (rape, murder, and other abuses) committed in his name.

Much to be said here. First, we see coverage of the ICC in our press and even U.S. government encouragement from the sidelines, but sometimes we are not reminded that the U.S. government boycotted the organization when it was created. The U.S. also waged a lengthy and energetic lobbying campaign sending delegations

("Article 98 Commissions") to other countries to woo them away from membership. There are good reasons for the U.S.'s opposition to the ICC structure, but our lobbying other countries should be part of the record.

Gbagbo, here pictured at a more serene moment in a Washington, DC, apartment in 1979, was known to a small circle of friends (including me!) as a gentle intellectual with a self deprecating sense of humor and a lively mind with the analytical skills of an historian. Accomplished historians look at events through many prisms, and teach us that drama derives from inner contradictions, nuances, shifting Rashomon points of view, and a sense that victims seldom get to write history, but likely should.

Laurent Gbagbo's very existence is an urgent challenge to what we think we know about human nature. In this regard we remain at an extremely primitive state. Recent research shows we are making pretty good progress in detecting compassion in rats, and communal planning by consensus among ants (the little guys at the picnic), whereas grasping traces of our own vile potential evades us nearly totally.

Urgentissimo, we should develop a science to detect and foresee these ominous transformations. Does a gentle academician become a murderous sadist from physiology? Chemistry? From emergence of previously undetected abnormalities? We'd better find out, and quick – or else.

The photos of Gbagbo's arrest (in April of 2011) are memorable. They show a bewildered fool at the end of his murderous spree, basically a petulant child with his candy or pacifier removed. Monsters (where and how are they produced out of normal human endeavors and development??) generally seem frail at the moment of their undoing. They draw no pity, nor should they. Even ridicule, which is tempting, is an insult to their victims.

Someone at the U.S. embassy in Abidjan chose Gbagbo in 1979 as a future intellectual leader of his country. The bromides on "leader

ship" polluting our bookstores and training centers embarrass in their cluelessness. The abundance of history's lessons on the fate of sadists, and ability of society to put up its dukes against them, seem to have no effect on the newly forming egomaniacs ready to send us all to hell until history teaches them their lesson yet again.

So the embassy had a good intuition of Gbagbo's potential, and I don't blame them for a prophesy gone awry.

The MDs, caregivers, dentists, and historians who litter the world currently demonstrate to us that teaching itself seems still to flounder in anachronistic imperfection. If the Founders were somehow brought for a visit to our present world, they would recognize the classroom, but little else in our environment. The classroom, a worthy institution, remains largely as it was in previous centuries and millennia. The bells and whistles enhance when they actually work.

The issue is not the space, the methodology, the accessibility of data. Seeing the seeds of monstrous crimes before they germinate, however, should be elevated to a new level of urgency. Calling for a new science, we'll need it from now on: let Creepology 101 and its clinical counterpart, Latent Deviantology, bloom in a thousand forms.

In a Name

December 15, 2011

This is not an obit, but George Whitman did die yesterday, age 98. For over a decade, people have been asking, "Is he still… alive?"

Not even close to being a relative of his, I did benefit from his cranky hospitality one winter day in 1970. I had just taken the cheap flight from Boston to Paris ($200 round trip) and debarked, jet-lagged, at Shakespeare and Company. It was too early in the day to go hunting for a hotel. Yes, I knew James Joyce had been there, and Hemingway, and all the others.

Whitman, the owner of the bookstore opposite Notre Dame Cathedral, noticed my same family name on the luggage tag, and took me over for the morning, storing my suitcase under a sort of desk near the front door of the shop, and sending me over to an ancient stuffed chair in the back to read or doze. I never heard another word from him, but saw his approving look as I picked up the suitcase later in the day. He knew one more American (of tens of thousands) had found his way fleetingly via Shakespeare and Company. This was what he was all about.

In the decades after World War II, Paris was still exotic to some, and was still largely French. Extremely flammable paraffin heaters broke the winter chill in the dusty shop, depending on where you were in the room. The city pulsed and lurched only blocks away, but Whitman's bookstore was an oasis among others in a city that still had some claim on world leadership, a Metropole of former colonies still sentimentally attached to a pretty stiff-necked and punitive mother country. Mainly what went on in the bookstore was the sound... of reading.

The recent Woody Allen film inserts a visual quote of this indefinable institution, a way station for Americans seeking escape from blandness. The airlines' price wars in the 1970s made these quests attainable for the middle class, and I actually saved money by closing out an apartment lease in Boston and spending two months in France. It would have cost more to take up another residence during those 60 days.

Many comments will come forth on the occasion of George Whitman's death, mine is only a brief reminiscence of a man who filled a role none other could or can.

A word more, on my name: it was given by a kindly, but semi-literate, customs officials at Ellis Island in the first decade of the twentieth century. My grandfather's old world name is still not known. A century later when I was spokesman at the U.S. Embassy in Haiti, journalists persistently misspelled my name as "Withman," I guess because they knew "th" is a diphthong in English. and "wh" didn't seem like one to them.

I pointed out the typo for a couple of months and then gave up the effort, as Haitians told me they knew my name better than I did.
Only in 2007 did I find a document in my late father's files, dated September 22, 1943 – an affidavit signed by the Honorable John H. Byrnes, Chief Justice of the City of New York, granting a name change from the original one given (Withman, sic) to a new one (Whitman). Thus, intuitive Haitians indeed knew my origins better than I did.

Quoting from the affidavit:

> ORDERED, that following the filing of the petition and or-
> der as hereinbefore directed and the publication of such or-
> der and the filing of proof of publication thereof, and of the
> service of a copy of said papers and of the order as herein-
> before directed, that on and after the first day of November,
> 1943, the petitioner shall be known by the name of SAM
> WHITMAN and by no other name.

George Whitman, if you are out there somewhere listening or
chuckling at this, thanks for the morning of chilly hospitality, and
for creating and sustaining a sanctuary of sorts – dusty, cluttered,
aimless, like life at its best. I wasn't a "Whitman" as much as you
were, but you gave me the benefit of the doubt. I will see about re-
laying the good turn to others.

An Ambassador Speaks

December 18, 2011

I want to think of Sir Nigel Sheinwald as "High Commissioner," but it seems the United States left the Commonwealth some years ago.

Washington's best conversationalist, Steve Clemons, introduced UK Ambassador Sheinwald to an audience of 80 on December 15, presenting the event as an "exit interview" in advance of Sir Nigel's retirement next month from the British Foreign Office.

"Conversation" was once a lofty art in the European tradition, and might be again under Steve Clemons's watch, outlasting and enduring the pollution of blabber we live in. Disclosure: I have no motive for sycophancy toward either of these two individuals, I only admire them. Clemons has an ongoing relationship with the New America Foundation, and is Washington editor-at-large for *The Atlantic*.

Ambassadors do perform exit interviews, sometimes in scripted language to the media of the countries they have lived in, or confidentially as "outbriefs" to their colleagues. The idea of offering an extemporaneous dialogue on the record was bold, innovative, snazzy.

Everyone wants to know what a British ambassador has to say about the United States after a four-year stint here, and following an earlier posting in 1983-87. His experience as advisor to Tony Blair from 2003 to 2007 makes the tale more alluring.

Sheinwald's steady intellect and affection for the United States shows us the "Special Relationship" which has been shorthand for U.S.-UK compatibilities since World War II. America's earliest literary development was judged by British standards well into the nineteenth century (Washington Irving, Hawthorne, the others), and into the twentieth (Henry James.) Americans are still enamored of the literature, history, and music of the British Isles, and go goofy over British royalty even with and despite our inculcated distrust of them.

Globalization and cultural diversity has underscored the proximity of the two cultures, not divided them. Sheinwald reminded us that even with a loss of power and influence, the United Kingdom remains as global in its outlook as it was when it ruled a vast empire. "If I were American, I'd be looking for more alliances," he said, "The UK may not be the only one around, but it does have global assets, and there aren't many others."

An ambassador's job is not to surprise or astonish, and Sheinwald lives this principle.

The most trying moments of his ambassadorship? "The BP oil spill in the Gulf of Mexico." The toughest problems we all face currently? "Pakistan and Afghanistan."

Our hopes of resolving them? "In some cases, your international partners have more confidence in you than you do yourselves."

Iran? "We've achieved some success with sanctions, but not yet a strategic change." The ambassador reminded us that UK, France, and Germany were first to impose sanctions, and that the United States was a follower, as were China and Russia. Point taken.

No surprises here, but the steady and affectionate glance of an outsider shows us that U.S. policy tautologies and the narcissism of commentators benefit from friendship and a fresh look.

Both the U.S. and Europe suffer from a "hemorrhaging of confidence," Sir Nigel said, ripping the bandage off the wound. To say that this is an exaggeration of our real circumstances indicates less rush to judgment of our triumphs and failures. We are reminded that Americans seek to solve problems, while the British outlive theirs. If indeed American power and influence is waning—as nearly all the periodicals now broadcast from their lead articles—then Britain is not a bad model to go by, for graceful and skillful adaptation to an hegemony lost. Americans were taught long ago that vast influence never lasts forever, but we never really believed it. Culture and influence can endure as power wanes. We knew that, but we forget.

The parallels are striking, and already form a chain of logic. The euphoria and idealism of Europe in the immediate post-War period are now given to cynicism and doubt, but likewise in the United States since Watergate. The 1980s brought a period of energy, optimism, bipartisanship, but then was checked by premature triumphalism following the fall of the Soviet Union.

Asked who his favorite presidents were, Sheinwald said into the microphone, "Steve, I told you before this conversation that I wouldn't answer that question." Clemons beamed, enjoying the joust and rising to Sheinwald's parry of Clemons's riposte.

Like Russians, Americans are very hard and very soft on themselves. The British ambassador shows us that the truth lies not in wallowing in the extremes, but lies between them. This is the tough love that friends show one another. As friendships among nations fray, each enduring one counts more. Finally, while American policy makers shy away from terms like "culture," and "intellect," friends remind us that these are virtues.

The effect of British culture on America? "Our actors seem to get all the roles in vampire movies."

Sir Nigel, we thank you for your friendship and your diction. We'll need such models if we are to weather the headwinds approaching.

All Power to the 164th

December 20, 2011

The State Department is not immune to budget woes. This employer of 22,000 (plus 31,000 Foreign Service National employees) has gone through a "seven percent exercise" nearly every budget cycle for the past dozen years, projecting what it would cut if it had to do so. Exercises are then actually implemented more often than not, to the dismay of the planners.

Asked at a public forum November 3 what resource he would be least willing to part with, planner and Deputy Assistant Secretary Bruce Wharton said without hesitation, "personnel."

Imagine, in an age of bells and whistles, a value placed on humans and their capacities. Blogster John Brown spoke July 24, 2010, of "The Newest Killer App for Public Diplomacy" – colorless, odorless, environmentally friendly, accessible to all, more effective than social media, and "TOTALLY FREE: face-to-face conversation!" The old and tested principles do sometimes work.

December 16, 52 new Foreign Service officers were sworn in as the 164th incoming "A-100" class in the State Department. Spirits were high, the camaraderie already established, the 52 psyched for consular assignments in parts of the world some never imagined.

One officer, trained in Swahili and French, was blindsided by an unexpected assignment to Shanghai. She quipped, "In the future I can serve in Africa with three African languages: French, Swahili, and Chinese."

Adaptability is the mode most favorable to a career of uncertainty, in an unpredictable world. The 52 go off with their flags in their buttonholes, cheerful for the chance to dust up their lives, ready to make virtuosic leaps to the unknown.

How close the group came to never existing as a class! Devastating cuts halted the intake of personnel and only the immediate needs of the consular service made them indispensable to the planners. It almost didn't happen.

Colin Powell's "Diplomatic Readiness Initiative," much vaunted in the early years of the 21st century, added tiny increments to a labor force decimated by doubt and retreat. The 164th may be one of the last for awhile, but Bruce Wharton's belief in them is the only sensible way forward.

Humans, states, bureaucracies renew themselves best by ceding to the new aspirants ready to explore without particular aim, to channel the nomadism of author Bruce Chatwin, and to favor questions and answers of others.

Like monks, they perform for us what we might not do ourselves, but wish we did. I do not lionize them, but I do thank them for taking over when others fall by the wayside. What we used to call civilization depends on them, their willingness to disrupt predictable patterns and endure long stretches of time beyond comfort.

Huzzah for the 164th. May their future counterparts join in, while America still has some relation to the world. Humans need not be far-seeing in the millions, in order for millions to benefit from those who are.

Christmas in Lunel

December 31, 2011

December 4, 2004, night flight Paris-Bamako. Malian journalists await for a week of training and encouragement to affirm, with an outsider, a free press in a country so poor it cannot even really falter. Sleep mask, ear stops, and I take my contrived sleep position so as to function for next day's press sessions.

Call it sleep, whatever happens at 30,000 feet over the Sahara with all precautions for the bits of energy conservation a traveler can muster.

As the plane began to bank and descend the next morning an hour before landing, the cabin crew distributed orange juice. As I was only half awake, the French passenger to my right helpfully asked me if I wanted some.

We spoke a bit, and swapped quick tales about what brought us to Bamako. "Journalism training," I said, still groggy. "And you?" I asked.

"Tomorrow I adopt a Malian child," She said. I found this pretty dramatic, and asked if she'd met the child on a previous trip.

"Never. We meet tomorrow at the orphanage," she said in the dry way the French have when they touch the perimeter of large and frightening emotions. We exchanged names and Bamako numbers. Laurence had been to Mali some months before as a tourist, and felt a strong and unexplainable connection to the land and its people.

"You come with courage," I said, and she teared up and confided in me (safer, always, to do so with a stranger) that she was a little terrified at what she was about to do, but also had removed all doubts that the adoption was her way forward.

We agreed to be in touch in Bamako at the end of the week, when my journalist certificates would be handed out from my side, and when the adoption papers would be ready from hers. Phone numbers in Bamako are not easy, but we did get in touch the following Thursday, and Laurence and her new Basile attended my closing session with the Malian journalists.

I improvised some blather, and introduced Laurence and the dozing toddler on her lap, "Africa does not lose a son, she gains a mother." Laurence surprised me by dissolving into tears. How unlike her dry control of four nights before.

Fast forward. Laurence planned her wedding July, 2008, with an old squeeze, Michel, in Nîmes, France. Based in Washington, I returned the invitation with the usual good wishes, and regrets that a trip to France wasn't in my agenda for the summer.

The response was immediate and firm, and came in the polite "*vous*" form: "Your presence is not optional. As you are to be designated as Basile's *parrain* (godfather), the ceremony can proceed only if you attend."

This left me with complications and consternation. Nevertheless I took the contemporary crucifixion pose on a longer night flight, and attended the wedding. It included a hay ride in the Camargue, and many toasts and short speeches. Laurence had a ton of friends and family, and they weren't about to forego her wedding as a 40-something bride giving this a try for her first time. The African child, possibly six by this time, was a curiosity for all. ("Possibly" because orphanages falsify the child's age downward, to draw in gullible and good-hearted Europeans.)

Who knows what goes on in the soul of a French woman at moments of adoption, marriage, advancement of destiny, heiress to an ancient culture where today remains fatalism alone, without the faith that once accompanied it.

I was snookered into the *cérémonie de parrainage*, which imposed serious obligations under French law. The formalities were held in the eighteenth century city hall in Nîmes, with officials in tricolor sashes, and cumbersome documents to sign in triplicate, before witnesses. No backing out. In France, I learned, *parrainage* is a not a matter to be taken lightly. The ceremony had the solemnity of a peace agreement among mutually distrusting states, though more fun than solemn.

Another fast forward, by three years, and an invitation for 2011 Christmas in France. We marked the seventh year of knowing each other, in a place called Lunel, half way between Nîmes and Montpellier. Oysters, champagne, *terrine de saumon*, some more rites of passage to make me temporarily French. I left the traditional *pâté de foie gras* to others.

With seven billion of us now, and almost everyone in some form of distress, a person has to do something to make life possible, even if for a few others. I refer to Laurence here, and her husband Michel. This is not kumbaya. A stark bifurcation leads to countdown to apocalypse, or survival. So has it always seemed, but now we have the data and photos to prove it.

Christmas afternoon, Laurence and I had a side talk about what can be expected of a person, in restoring dwindling resources to growing numbers of people with needs, and by the way, with the ability to take things from us when they must. Mumbo jumbo aside, we are in dire straits, with no easy way out. As to individual guidance – at our luckiest we receive invitations in the mail, marking the way forward. More often, we must divine the path ahead and make the best of it. QED, whether we may make it through the Long March to reverse global depletion or, rather, shrivel and die like little fools.

Zelig at INF

January 19, 2012

The Intermediate-Range Nuclear Forces Agreement of 1987 was one of the few dramatic advances for human survival in an otherwise murderous twentieth century. I didn't make any of it happen, but I was a fly on the wall in its various phases.

October 11-12, 1986, Reykjavik Summit – the long faces of Reagan and Gorbachev as they exited the Hofdi House. So near, yet so far, to dismantling the most destructive arsenals ever assembled by humans.

The following week, Jack Matlock came to Copenhagen where I taxied him around to Danish officials. Matlock was the third individual in the room at Hofdi House. As Junior Officer in Denmark, I was his sounding board for the week.

"Do you realize how close we came to the first time in history that two major powers voluntarily eliminated an entire class of weapons?" I absorbed but could not augment his excitement.

And, "The ambassadorship in Moscow, I'd like to do that one day."

And so he did, the only one publicly praised and acknowledged by the greatest of them all, George F. Kennan.

Then came the Venice Economic Summit, in June of 1987. I set up a folding card table at the temporary U.S. press center on Lido Beach, armed with a landline and a pen, nothing more. Seven thousand journalists hovered in the city, desperate for scraps of news to report. No minister or head of state had much to say, and the pool reports said spiteful things like, "She wore a red dress with white brocaded collar..."

Sitting at my humble card table I took a call from Alexei Adzhubei, a Soviet TV journalist. In pretty good English he asked for an interview with SecState George Shultz, who hadn't even arrived yet in town. I noted the request on a torn half of an envelope, and stuck it in the hotel room slot of Charles Redman, Shultz's spokesman.

Mirabile dictu, Shultz chose Adzhubei for his only interview of the week. He wanted to tell the Soviet people that the two countries were close to an INF agreement, and Soviet TV was the way he wanted to do it. The rules were simple: no editing of the interview from the Soviet side, and the questions had to be submitted in advance.

Seven thousand journalists didn't yet know they had been stiffed by the U.S. SecState. I knew I'd be dead meat if they ever found out I was the facilitator.

All the gondolas and *vaporettos* had been commandeered by the G-7. We found one remaining one, and made it to the Cipriani hotel on San Giorgio Maggiore Island with the Soviet journalist and his camera crew of two.

Hastily on the 20-minute crossing, we worked out the interview format: I would write the journalist's questions in English on 3 x 5 cards for Secretary Shultz, the journalist would ask them in Russian. Shultz would answer in English, and the final cut would have Russian voice-over for the whole ten minutes. OK, it was my idea.

The journalists thought this was a fine way to proceed, and we worked out the wording of the questions on a bobbing gondola as we approached the island...

Shultz, too, liked the format. The TV interview reached an audience of about 100 million. I kept a low profile, aware of the rage and jealousy of the 7,000 other journalists famished for news and never getting any of their own.

In winter of 1987 I was sent as a stagehand for the final negotiations of Shultz and Shevardnadze, putting the finishing touches and initials on an INF agreement.

February 4, 1987. Gloomy, rainy day in Geneva. The two FoMins met in a chalet while 30 journalists and I waited outside in the freezing rain. Hours passed, and most gave up and left the press area in search of warmth or hot chocolate or better news. By the time the two Foreign Ministers exited to the deck of the chalet to announce their success, only a dozen journalists remained.

Shultz said to the remaining cameras in his unambiguous American plainspeak, "Why are we shaking hands? Because we have just agreed, for the first time in history, to eliminate an entire class of lethal weapons. This is a great step forward." You could see that Shultz and Shevardnadze were fond of each other.

I jumped onto the press bus to help get the journalists to their filing center, in the days before iPhones and BlackBerries. We all checked with each other to get the wording exactly right.

Paul Nitze did a backgrounder for American press late in the afternoon. We sat on a comfortable rug in a wood-lined study like kindergartners, and heard about the hard numbers of missile reductions and the arithmetic of partial disarmament.

The final draft of the treaty was signed by Reagan and Gorbachev on December 8, 1987. History indicates that Ronald Reagan may have genuinely wanted a denuclearized world, and might have had one back in Reykjavik but for his insistence or intransigence on the Strategic Defense Initiative – "Star Wars." INF was a small step in that direction, and led to the accommodations between the two superpowers at the end of the Cold War in 1991.

More steps needed to be taken, never mind that rogue states and non-state actors might soon get access to these monstrous killing stocks. Having more of them benefits no one. Just leave us with ten or so to destroy all forms of life, it's fully adequate.

INF was an achievement now seldom remembered. The current pickles we are in may come from lack of interlocutors as we had back then. Now we seek contact with the Taliban, maybe from nostalgia of the days of face-to-face table talks from the 1980s. The lessons of INF may yet cut some corners to release us from another policy nightmare. Plenty of fools populate the stage, but not many who want mutual destruction as a strategy.

"In Some Village, An Idiot Goes Missing…"

January 23, 2012

No, this is not a commentary on the season's presidential primaries. The quote comes from an anonymous wag's version of how to low-rank an employee's evaluation without directly naming the employee. The latter would be "actionable" commentary, and could lead to ugly law suits.

Back to the topic: there is something ingratiating about the concept of the "village idiot," which refers as much to the village as to the "idiot." Villages are mysterious and ancient entities, and seem to be the naturally intended units of human habitation.

The concept has negatives and positives. *"Pueblo pequeño, infierno grande,"* says the Spanish proverb, noting that villagers and their gossip can be corrosive and cruel when they set their minds to it. Just as often, they have their ways of making accommodations with one another, for survival's sake. See *Il Campiello* of Carlo Goldoni (1756), for examples of the latter.

May, 2006. I was hiking near a tiny village up-country in Cameroon, somewhere near the Sahel city of Garoua, but far removed
from any viable crossroads. Villagers came to greet me, asking for
nothing, offering only smiles and welcomes. Accompanying them
was a man in wrist manacles and chains, with heavy clinking metal, thicker than the ones you'd see dangling from a motorcycle. It
seemed straight out of the movie *Amistad*. The man walked in labored paces, heaving around with him the weight of two meters of
iron links and chains under the manacles.

I was taken aback at this time warp, and thought "slave," because
this was my only point of reference for a man in rags and chains
being led around by others.

All were cordial, including the prisoner-or-whatever, who greeted
me and asked if I might have 1000 FCFA for him, the equivalent of
two dollars U.S. No problem in passing this on, and he received
the currency with an elegant bow. Yet another literary flashback: I
thought *Benito Cereno* – perhaps the real prisoner here was myself.
The villagers chatted amiably with me. I took one of them aside and
asked about their neighbor in irons.

"Oh, that's Pierre," one said discreetly as an aside, "He's a little unpredictable and sometimes beats children if we don't restrain him."
Then I saw in perspective: African villages don't have psychiatric
services (duh), nor are they cruel when they can find a way around
it. When a villager steps out of line, the village finds pragmatic
ways of keeping the social order with a minimum of hurt. Punitive
acts are not in their inventory of social remedies, but self protection
and social integration are. The neighbor Pierre was included in village activities and honored as a full, participating member of the
social fabric, though kept in chains just to be sure.

With limited resources, this village near Garoua, Cameroon, found
its ways to ensure social peace and village well-being. I saw no
spite or contempt for the man in chains, only acceptance and inclu-
sion – though with restraint.

African solutions might serve as our own future models as our institutions wither from budgetary trauma. We could pay close attention and heed their examples of human self-defense against locos.

Perhaps a society should be judged not by the number of "village idiots," as those will always populate the landscape. Rather, the clever villages integrate their eccentrics with acceptance, acknowledgement of their status as humans, and with vigilant awareness of their irrational and maybe mostly harmless disruptions of the civic harmony.

Open Season on War Crimes

February 7, 2012

This just in, from recent critics of drone strikes, Guantanamo, and suspension of habeas corpus: we are in a new equation and things are better than we thought.

Marking the seventieth anniversary of the Wannsee conference sketching out Europe's Final Solution for the elimination of Jews (January 20, 1942), the National Holocaust Memorial Museum held a public forum February 2 with Morton Abramowitz, William Shawcross, David Scheffer, and Harold Hongju Koh on future prosecutions of war crimes. This time, we are talking about non-state actors who terrorize and kill random populations for twisted purposes more of perceived revenge than ideology. Times change.

The speakers were, respectively, a long-respected journalist for the *Washington Post*, a British author and son of the leading British prosecutor at the Nuremberg Trials, Clinton's negotiator at the ad hoc tribunals gathering in perpetrators from the former Yugoslavia and Rwanda (and also the lead of the American delegation in Rome, 1998, which yielded the International Criminal Court), and a Yale law professor and Supreme Court nominee who now serves as legal counsel to the Department of State.

Some in the audience were stunned to hear from these highly regarded authorities, that circumstances have changed since the Bush era abuses, and that some of the means used toward combating terrorism—previously out of bounds—are now acceptable.

Shawcross's new book on the prosecution of Khalid Sheikh Mohammed releases some of the hammerlocks on methods of prosecution which were no-no's to some, under the Bush administration.

The panel mainly agreed on the following: Guantanamo is now equipped to dispense valid justice and prosecution apparatus, and is good to go as a legal entity; targeted drone strikes (even of U.S. citizens abroad) are now legitimate; empirical data shows that human rights abuses are generally in decline world-wide; the assassination of Osama bin Laden was desirable in both content and style; and American exceptionalism is no longer a dirty word or concept. No small astonishment. Koh, a leading critic in 2004-2009 of the Bush practice of extra-legal detention of suspected terrorists, and enhanced interrogation techniques, now sees these practices as within the parameters of legitimate national self-defense (though with "zero tolerance on torture"). Scheffer is "delighted" at the killing of Osama bin Laden even if the Navy Seals acted on orders to kill rather than capture him. Though a European, Shawcross asserted the validity, strength and importance of American supremacy as the best means available to pursue interdiction and trial in an anarchic world, *faute de mieux*.

The strength of the Holocaust Memorial Museum is its focus on prevention of future human rights abuses, with a reasoned avoidance of singling out cultures, nations, or ethnic groups for unshakeable blame from one generation to the next. This clear thinking is what has made it a national treasure and magnet for millions of visitors per year.

Though the perpetrators of 9/11 were never accused of genocide, their crimes now figure as elements of a new threat to human existence and social order. Though the Holocaust Museum was set up to see how to prevent focused genocide, the new threat has more to do with a new species of malicious but random killings.

I am not the only one to have missed a leap in reasoning, from the harsh criticism of the Bush administration in its reliance on extra-legal, enhanced interrogations, GITMO detentions, and extraordinary renditions of suspects to dark prisons. Highly respected critics now say that the nature of the threat calls for freer use of the means available to combat it. One of the panelists said he had specific evidence of water boarding yielding valuable information which saved hundreds and maybe thousands of civilians' lives.

Harold Koh, who in 2008 said to PBS, "…We're in the last days of a dying policy here. …Guantanamo is unacceptable," now points to the reinforced legal apparatus of Guantanamo. GITMO admittedly was chosen by the Bush administration for detention of suspected illegal combatants, because of its location outside of U.S. territory: this created a loophole or an ambiguity to dodge the U.S.'s obligations under the Geneva Conventions of 1949 to provide specific rights to enemy captives. But the default has now flipped, and we are to accept this mechanism for disarming combatants out of uniform, with habeas corpus suspended until the end of the present conflict, even if we don't know if this moment will come in our lifetimes.

David Scheffer assures us that U.S. refusal to ratify the Rome Statute of 1998 and become a member of the ICC is no longer an impediment. He cites a "mood change" which allows close cooperation and collaboration by the United States with the international body.

It takes one's breath away. I am not trying to be surly – these individuals have earned credibility in confronting abuses. We are now invited to consider alternatives previously associated with the Inquisition, and with techniques that seemed to violate laws of war and peace.

Harold Koh got the last word: "As an Asian American, I find it curious that the nation which was willing to use nuclear weapons to kill tens of thousands of civilians in Asia, now picks at the validity of the use of targeted drone strikes that take out those who would kill us."

How can one argue with him, now or before? Time to look at all the criticism of Bush human rights abuses, and consider options never before permitted by international law. Color me puzzled, naked of prior suppositions, and humbled by new twists and paradigms I'd never heard of before. It doesn't seem right, but I'll have one more look at it all, as we all should.

Stalin Without the Bullets

February 9, 2012

She was recommended for promotion and assigned to a high-profile post in the Middle East. The Department sent her off to learn a hard language, investing about a quarter of a million dollars in the effort (consider her salary, the language teacher's pay, the meals and incidental expenses, the cost of leaving a post unoccupied for eight months.)

Not so fast. Someone unnamed had a tropical fantasy and imagined her bedding down with locals at a previous posting, shouting out state secrets at moments of spasmic contentment.

Thus the harassment began, never mind habeas corpus, facing the accuser and the rest of it, as her presumed offense had to do with internal rules of the bureaucracy, nor any civil legal code.

Interrogated overseas without warning, she said, "If this is the direction you are going in, I'd rather do this back in Washington, with legal counsel." They answered, "Then this means you might have something to hide."

In fact this all did happen, I won't say when or where or to whom.

The Washington interrogation a month later lasted three hours and came out inconclusive. The pro bono attorney said to her afterward, "I can't really tell what they were getting at."

A year later, after the language training, the movers came one day to pick up her household goods. The phone rang and she reached over cardboard boxes to get the news that her onward assignment was broken.

Her promotion was kept on hold until the case could be resolved. Her security clearance was suspended.

The System reassigned her to a sensitive post in a hot spot, even with her clearance blocked. The System does not permit this of itself, but it did in this case, because she was needed.

She did dynamic work in her new post, and uncovered human rights abuses no one had noticed before. Campuses, governments, and journalists—and a few movie stars—took up the cause. The struggle galvanized well wishers of different persuasions, and led to political changes for the better.

Still, her promotion was blocked and she was passed over for other assignments.

The adjudication—in her favor—came a year later when her legs began to fail and her face twitched from stress. It could be my imagination, but I think she lost some control of the muscles in her cheek below the left eye socket.

Health and youth and hope spent, she received the letter telling her the investigation was completed, and she would get retroactive pay for the delayed promotion. Even with the increase, she was well below the senior threshold.

She filed her retirement papers the next month and packed for home, though "home" was an elusive concept for her at the time.

The gents suspected of bedding down with her went into action years later when a natural disaster hit their country and they were called upon to save lives, and did so.

On an average day, the Department has about one hundred law cases on its hands. Most of them come down in favor of the plaintiff and against the Department. This, even before real litigation takes place and they settle out of court – thanks to a self-correcting mechanism within the System. Long live corrections, but they are expensive.

The more cost-effective method would be to line up the accused and just dispatch them.

Cheaper, even, would be to give them some trust in the first place. People are worse and better than they seem. Leave them alone and get on with business, if you want anything left in "accounts payable," or any restraint on the dark hearts of the persecutors.

Lavrov Crunched

February 13, 2012

Russian Foreign Minister Sergei Lavrov led the charge February 5 to nix and veto a UN Security Council resolution condemning Syria's Assad for killing his own citizens. China followed it, but had less to say about this seemingly despicable act.

"Disgusting!" said U.S. PermRep Susan Rice, in a refreshing departure from bland, diplomatic language.

Karen DeYoung and Liz Sly said in the February 11 *Washington Post*, "Russia's veto appears to have emboldened the government to unleash even greater force in its effort to crush the uprising…"

In a world of ambiguities, it comes as a ray of light to see foolishness and evil make a rare joint appearance. Russia gets money from Syria's Bashar Assad, and benefits from having access to the Syrian port of Tartus, fulfilling Catherine the Great's dream of warm-water ports for the Russian navy.

The joy, seeing the perpetrator's flag trashed by angry mobs in cities around the world, and the thought that Russia has gone double-or-nothing at the gaming table, for once betting on the wrong cards. It may not be quite so simple. Remember the period of kidnappings in Beirut in the 1970s and '80s, when Soviets seemed immune to the factional violence. Maybe urban legend, but it seems that the USSR had found the formula to success: capture the Lebanese brother of the kidnapper of a Soviet official, and arrange to send the left ear of the brother by FedEx equivalent to the kidnappers, with a note: "...And we have the rest of him. Deliverable in a plastic bag by Wednesday unless you release our captive."

And thus, no more kidnappings of Soviets during that very stressful period.

Let us imagine, just hypothetically, that even the most cynical Russian official would rather not see their man Assad drenched further in the blood of uninvolved citizens of Homs, and look a bit more closely at this faux pas of the February 4 veto.

Russia is of course an emasculated power since 1992, yet it remains the largest country in the world in land mass. Here is what Lavrov actually said last week, rather steamed at the whole predicament: "Those who get angry are hardly ever right."

"Efforts to stop violence have to be met with dialogue by all the political forces."

"There is not one single, but many sources of violence."

Maddening stuff, but does it sound familiar? Who would want to be Lavrov at this moment? Presumably he acted on orders from above – though his own inner soul, if any, may be in alignment with those orders. We don't know for sure.

Could Russia have done otherwise, or should it have? For this there is no clear answer, but consider the Bear beleaguered, outflanked, outgunned, outmaneuvered by a NATO only recently released from non-aligned opprobrium. This could give a Russian official a stomachache.

It could be that they well deserve the sudden hatred of wide swaths of the Arab world for their cynical acts and double dealing. But let us not fall into complacency; we were the punching bag for many decades, and could become so again. As we consider this, we see 16 Americans on the docket in Cairo for possible "crimes" against the Arab spring, 25 percent "approval" rate for the U.S. among the Egyptian public, and the wells of hatred for us will not run dry any time soon.

Amid these dreadful events and the predicament we face as well ("US sees few good options in Syria" – *Washington Post*, February 11), we may have more in common with Russia than today's news implies. Arab countries have subliminal memories of our many vetoes in the Security Council, and are not about to give us a pass for them.

It must have given contentment to Soviets throughout the 1970s and '80s to see the United States as Bad Guy in much of the Middle East. Now, inevitably, it is their turn.

If we were to match the overlap in our interests with theirs and see how we might work together to ride and support the Arab spring, all might benefit. Schadenfreude is tempting, but joint actions could produce a win-win, no guarantees.

Russia, February 5, 2012, your bad. Now to catch them on the rebound, and see what we might possibly do together.

Shovels to Anguissa

February 16, 2012

I had just moved into the Public Affairs Office in the embassy in Yaoundé. Public Affairs offices build links to the civil society, deter youth from terrorism, and highlight values consistent with the U.S. versions of democracy, human rights, and free markets.

A young delegation called "Fondation Conseil Jeune" came to visit. They brought a laptop to demonstrate their organization's structure, mission statement, and plan for expansion. They were energetic and bright.

"We want to hold a conference to promote democracy and draw on our sister organizations from the other provinces."

"That's great," I said. "Thanks for letting me know."

Then they handed me the estimated bill and suggested my office front the costs of the hall rental, meals, transport, and hotel rooms for those who would have to travel to the capital.

"But, to do what?" I asked. Something about the plan didn't seem right.

"Well, discuss democracy."

I said, "You support democracy?" Yes, they said. "Well so do I. Then there isn't much of a discussion. Nice to meet you."

This wasn't what the group had planned. Here was the flaw in the plan: people would be fed, housed, profess a faith, and then return home. The obstacles to democracy (most of the country's government and much of its private sector) wouldn't even be in the room. It was good funded palaver, but not an action that could produce an outcome.

"This is the Public Affairs Section, isn't it?" one said challenging me, but with dignity. Right, I said.

"Isn't it your job to support this type of activity?"

"Not exactly," I said. "We develop links with civil society, and support lasting structures."

"But this is what we bring to you."

"I don't do conferences," I said. "Not this time. Can you tell me the problem you need fixed?"

They looked at one another, maybe wondering if they were in some sort of danger.

"We want democracy in our country."

"Me too," I said. "But that is not a problem, it's a wish."

"Problem?" they said. "There is no transparency, no accountability here."

"I should be clearer," I said. "In your daily life, what stands in your way?"

One of those who hadn't yet spoken said, "Our neighborhood in Anguissa has no water. The pipes were put in thirty years ago, but now they're clogged, and the government does nothing."

There I saw the opening. "Then you need drain pipes cleared, is that it?" They all nodded yes.

"Then let's go out and clear them. Together. You tell me when to show up with a shovel, and I'll be there."

The group looked at my blue blazer on a hook by the door, and the diplomatic title hanging on the wall. I knew it didn't exactly fit a paradigm. From previous posts, I felt that too many conferences achieved nothing much for the embassy or the community. Maybe it was my mood that day.

The group was disconcerted but retreated for future friendly assault. I knew the funds in my budget were tiny compared to what they imagined. I liked the group but didn't really expect to hear from them again.

Ten days later they called my bluff: in an artfully composed email, they challenged me to show up with a shovel the following Saturday. They attached an impressive website describing their organization.

I grabbed the Deputy Chief of Mission and his two sons, and showed up with gym shoes, shorts, and shovels. Joined by about 50 young people from the community, we had the drains cleared within half a day. Presto: running water for the first time in 20 years. Press coverage may have shamed the local authorities, we don't really know.

Later we held the democracy conferences – Fondation Conseil Jeune made all the arrangements, paid the bills themselves, and turned to me only to cover the cost of reprinting the Cameroonian Constitution for wide distribution. Glad to do it. Spirits were high.

Now, six years later, the Foundation still exists and carries on bravely, though democracy in their country has had some nasty reversals. It seems they are in it for the long haul.

Churchill said, "Better to jaw-jaw than war-war." But he meant jaw-jaw with the opponent in the room. When such luxuries are beyond reach, better to shovel shit today and then jaw-jaw tomorrow.

Chekhov's Garden

February 20, 2012

It took thirty years because he agreed to do it posthumously, but John Lewis Gaddis's biography of U.S. diplomat George F. Kennan did come out a few months ago (New York: Penguin, 2011). Nothing much to add to the avalanche of positive reviews, all of them merited. As Gaddis himself says, he was Kennan's biographer for longer than Boswell was Johnson's. Not an immodest claim, just a statement of the truth.

One anecdote stood out, from Gaddis's discussion of the book at the Woodrow Wilson Center February 15, in Washington DC. Kennan was a motherless child who loved Anton Chekhov. Kennan, who wanted to be remembered as Chekhov's biographer (the greatest writer after Shakespeare, he said), never got around to writing it. This is not a random detail in getting to know American's greatest strategist of the twentieth century.

Chekhov, a medical doctor who understood the tuberculosis that would fell him, carried on even so with his writings, and poignantly, with the planting of his garden in the dacha he had built in Yalta in 1898, after the success of *The Seagull*, and his own father's death. Chekhov devoted much of his remaining energies to the dacha's garden, knowing he would never see the results of his labors.

Though he lived 101 years, Kennan imitated this action in his Pennsylvania farm in the town of East Berlin, moved by his role model's devotion, and afflicted all his life by the death of his mother only three months after his birth. Her death, in 1904, eerily coincided with Chekhov's.

Lacking a mother of his own, Kennan found surrogates in his sister Jeannette, and eventually with his Norwegian wife, Annelise, to whom Gaddis's biography is dedicated. However, Kennan's public grief in 1999 indicated that he never really recovered from the loss. Here is Gaddis on the subject. Th text below is Gaddis's. The quotation marks indicate Gaddis's citing of the original Chekhov text.

> June, 1999, a distinguished elder statesman, at ninety-five failing physically but fully in command mentally, suddenly sheds tears as he recalls Anton Chekhov's haunting story "The Steppe," about a boy of nine traveling with a group of peasants across a vast Russian landscape. The boy misses his mother, "understanding neither where he was going nor why," and trying to grasp the meaning of stars at night, only to find that they "oppress your spirit with their stillness," hinting at "that solitariness awaiting us all in the grave."

Why Chekhov, why the emphasis on loneliness, and why then, the containment policy which may have rescued the human race from nuclear annihilation and also accurately saw the Soviet Union's demise 40 years before it happened?

Kennan visited Chekhov's dacha and garden in 1937, 32 years after the latter's death and 39 years after its planting. He was moved to create a replica at his own Pennsylvania farm, which he bought in 1942.

Channeling Kennan, Gaddis explains the whole thing in a phrase: "We must be gardeners, not mechanics, in approaching world affairs." Gardeners foster growth but do not force it. In opposing a foe, Kennan says—through Gaddis—that gentleness, patience, and persistence are the qualities that yield results. The garden is no mere metaphor.

When Chekhov moved into his dacha in 1898, it was bare, denuded of vegetation. The stunning results showed only years later, with the results of patience and persistence. He planted trees including mulberry, cherry almond, peach, cypress, citrus, acacia, and birch. A semi-tame migrating crane landed on his shoulder during its yearly trips to and from the south. Knowing he would never see the finished garden did not daunt him.

How, in finding the right way to stare down the Soviet threat, did Kennan maintain a quiet and human strength? The truth is in the inversion of these counter-intuitively linked elements: the human, through loneliness, and the gardener's illogical passion for growth outside of himself, finds the Grand Strategy. Rivalry, arms races, power struggles, even the survival of the Earth itself, derive from a single person's need for a place within the Earth's embrace.

Gaddis said February 15, "Kennan lived to see the fruits of the seeds he planted, Chekhov was not as fortunate. Chekhov's planting 'took root' in the mind of Kennan, and played a role in saving civilization."

Thanks, John Lewis Gaddis, for your own persistence and disinterested gaze, to bring this linkage clearly to the rest of us.

Following the elusive patterns of a human spirit remains as compelling as knowing the number and location of the enemy's ICBMs, or the pyromania of those who would attack us today.

An Artist's Finest Moment

February 22, 2012

In 1988, Joseph-Francis Sumégné, here pictured, began collecting and sifting trash in the streets of Douala for his magnum opus. An untutored sculptor, he saw patterns and spirits in *objets trouvés*: coke bottle caps, empty coffee tins, discarded batteries, wicker fans, cloth remnants, and a thousand other items from the litter choking the streets of Cameroon's gritty seaport.

He tinkered with his mountain of junk in his workshop, fitting together items that had no previous fit for one another. Perhaps only an animist who sees life in rocks and tree stumps could have even imagined Sumégné's astonishing achievement after 15 years of solitary work. But the outcome was clear and impactful for anyone who stepped into a room with the nine larger-than-life sculptures that resulted.

Born purely of junk, the Nine Notables gathered in a traditional circle to tell tales around the evening camp fire, take decisions, serve as judge and jury when the village required. The installation, depicting the judge, jury, city council, university, and healing clinic

of any traditional village in Cameroon's Western provinces, struck the viewer in the solar plexus, as if Goya, Daumier, Dali, Rodin, Holbein, Puvis de Chavannes, Raphael, Picasso had somehow rethought all their work together and taken up media never before used to catch the human spirit.

The street junk, like keys of an organ, became mere levers to produce expressions of fear, irony, compassion, ridicule, slapstick, distress, contentment, and power in the nine figures, each with a character distinctly, even violently, different from the others.

No one who has walked among these statues will forget the strength of the experience.

Different in genre and certainly in locale, Sumégné's versatility is Chaucerian. The strivings, stumblings, the rhetoric and bombast and *gros comique* of his figures seized the viewer with the magnitude of human endeavor and folly. Cruelty nowhere present, the gigantic figures swept up the visitor in their power, pathos, humor, vanity, and attitudes which lacked even a vocabulary to describe them.

Sumégné was a playful and flamboyant spirit. He was a virtuoso of the welding torch and had the perfect pitch of silent music that ran through his work. No slouch, he labored over the Nine Notables for 15 years, rendering individual artworks to reach universal impact, traveling to France, Japan, Senegal, and Gabon.

Ambassador Niels Marquardt understood the power and charm of the collection, and ordered us in the embassy to get the work into the inner atrium of the New Embassy Compound when it was inaugurated in 2006. The pieces had to be dismantled in Douala, brought by truck and set up once again in the artist's vision in the foyer of the fancy new U.S. Embassy building in Yaoundé.

And what an installation it was. Terrifying, exhilarating, inexplicably bewilderingly powerful. Everyone who saw it felt its power.

A Marine guard responsible for the well-being of the building had been on annual leave, and wasn't present during the week of the installation. He was spooked in the midnight emptiness of the hall. In the dim light he found the figures imminently menacing. He unholstered his loaded revolver and shot into the Notables, spooked at their presence and also cognizant of his responsibilities as a caretaker of the new building's secure integrity.

Shots flew through the shadowy night to keep these ghostly presences from disturbing the tranquility of the embassy. The bullets pierced the Notables and lodged in the walls of the brand new atrium.

The next morning no one had the heart to admonish the Marine who had done this. Anyone could have done the same, in the sinister glow of his lonely night watch.

A few weeks later, I broke the news to the sculptor that his work had been damaged by bullet holes. He asked why, and I explained. He exclaimed with pure joy that no artist could succeed to such a degree in creating verisimilitude. His face turned to happiness and joy.

And of course he was right, the ability to convince the viewer of a reality in artifice is the artist's greatest aspiration. A master sculptor, an acute observer.

Remember the actor in South Dakota in the 1880s who played an evil Richard III, and who was shot and killed by an overreacting cowboy in the audience. The actor and the killer (later convicted of second degree murder and hanged) were buried in adjoining graves, acknowledged in the tombstones as "the perfect actor and the perfect audience."

Stolen Sandwiches

March 4, 2012

Late 2002, and we knew the Unites States would attack Saddam Hussein's Iraq. We were instructed to prepare world opinion for the onslaught.

I probably shouldn't have been at the table, but was, the day Under-secretary for Public Affairs (U/S) talked about a video to produce, proving that Saddam Hussein stole food from Iraqi children. I had flashbacks to Francisco Goya's series *Los Disparates*, or the *Pinturas negras*, the one of Saturn devouring his own son.

"Your reactions?" the U/S said to the twelve of us around the table. All nodded assent. "Any other comments?" she added, trying to start a discussion. No one would have any of it.

I took the bait. "Do we actually have video footage for this purpose?" I asked. I imagined the ideal sequence: Saddam Hussein grabbing an egg salad sandwich out of the mouth of an Iraqi child. I thought, "It will be a public diplomacy miracle if there is such a shot in an archive somewhere."

"Of course we do," she answered, glancing at me from across the table. All nodded assent.

She continued, "And the Kurds. Hussein gassed the Kurds, it was a horrible human rights violation."

Mouths all shut, eyes down.

"Comments?" she said. There were none.

"No comments at all?" she added.

I said, "The chemical attacks against the Kurds took place in 1991, eleven years ago. Maybe we have some more recent footage we might use?"

The U/S peered at me again from the far end of the table. Her eyes turned to narrow slits. "WHO ARE YOU?" she asked menacingly. I gave my name, rank, and office affiliation. "Are you trying to prevent this project from going forward?" she said.

I answered, "No, I'm trying to help. It will be a great video, and even better if we ask the questions that could be on the minds of foreign publics viewing the film."

She jotted something down on her legal pad. Those colleagues who dared, glanced at me with compassion for a fallen comrade.

And as Virginia Woolf would have said ("Lappin and Lapinova"), that was the end of that career. That phase of it, anyway.

The Devil's Due

March 8, 2012

Now that we've abandoned the people of Homs to unimaginable suffering, it is time to reflect on the meaning of the debacle.

Beleaguered towns have been rendered to the Devil since beyond memory. We drift into bromides of wishful thinking – "It's not if, but when, the regime collapses..." but the inconvenient truth is that the Devil has outsmarted us once again.

In the previous century the term "Red Cross" lifted hopes universally, but now even the rebranded "Red Crescent" is spurned by sadistic authorities, who since March 2 have kept them from entering Baba Amr, a concentration of misery, stress, and pain in the Syrian city.

The defection yesterday of Deputy Oil Minister Abdo Hussameddin raises hopes, but isolation for the Assad regime may only render it more intransigent.

The *Washington Post* editorial of March 3 made vague appeals for "a credible threat of force." But oil on the fire can take more victims in a circle of contempt for humans. This is the position of the Obama Administration, reinforced in the past three days by Secretary of State Hillary Clinton, Secretary of Defense Leon Panetta, and Joint Chiefs of Staff Chairman General Martin Dempsey. Extremely bad luck for the Syrian opposition: al Qaeda has gotten into the act, and will snatch weapons meant for the citizens' defense.

Even in our strongest moments of cynicism, Americans are anguished by others' catastrophes, tantalized by wishes for happy solutions. Never mind the sobering moments in recent history – we still cannot stomach resignation to cruelty, stupidity, and unmerited suffering. Again we have our "Oslo moment" – the massacres of August, 2011 which threw a kindly nation out of innocence. Like a reptile's missing tail, hope grows back, and restores good wishes and gullibility.

Here is more of what was said in the March 1 Senate hearing on Syria: with 9,000 civilians now killed, al Qaeda from Iraq is benefiting from Syria's instability. Though 137 nations voted in the UNGA to condemn President Bashar Al Assad's actions, twelve disagreed. Syrians themselves are "on the fence" over whether to risk the overthrow of a regime most of them loathe.

Our capable Assistant Secretary for Near Eastern Affairs, Jeffrey Feltman, says that Assad's "tipping point" will come, but has not yet manifested itself. The task of the United States is to "accelerate," not create, the tipping point.

The admirable Ambassador Robert Ford notes that shortages of cooking oil and heating fuel, while affecting primarily Syrian civilians, are putting unsustainable pressure on the regime. He assures the committee that the Syrian opposition are committed to rule of law and a democratic development. He says that the first word on everyone's lips is "dignity," when asked what they wish for their country.

Senator Bob Corker (R-TN), presumably violating rules of confidentiality, says that a classified briefing of the February 29 made the opposite case, claiming that the uprising is all about ethnic infighting. Rashomon. Same phenomena, opposite conclusions.

Bob Casey (D-PA), expressing a frustration that most Americans would share (and echoed in recent appeals by John McCain), says that merely passing one resolution after another will get us nowhere, and will go down in history as cowardice and inaction. But Assistant Secretary Feltman convincingly reasons, "For more aggressive action, we would need a larger international consensus than the one we have now."

Now U.S. Central Command Marine General James Mattis says of Assad, "I think he will continue to employ heavier and heavier weapons on his people… It will get worse before it gets better." President Obama calls the situation "heartbreaking and outrageous," but even the nettlesome Representative John Boehner (R-OH) agrees that "the situation in Syria is pretty complicated," and that good options do not now exist for United States intervention, either unilaterally or multilaterally (*Washington Post*, March 7).

So Gulliver is roped down by Lilliputians, and can only writhe in a perfect confinement. For now, at least.

Had we but been pacifist consistently throughout, we could fathom the sorry fate of others. But we didn't, and we used might to affirm right, which was our own version of loss of innocence. We exercised whack-a-mole since our last legal effort to right the wrongs of the world, i.e., World War II. Our forays since then have spent the whacks down to the last one. It recalls George F. Kennan's dinosaur, who "…lays about him with such blind determination that he not only destroys his adversary but largely wrecks his native habitat."

Unbearable, the Devil's current triumph, and our incapacity to stop the killing. Our stance may have elements of strength as well as failure, a grip on how history shows our track record in imposing good over evil. Knowing what we cannot hope to do may be a sign of maturity, emerging from a sea of reckless words in the current domestic political discourse.

There may be decency in our foundations after all, hence our distress at Syrians' suffering and at our own failure to alleviate them. The decency may lead to wishful thinking, empty solace, and an inverse perversity of the knowledge of our limits. It may even be the morphine of self-delusion. But anguish is one basis for wisdom; and wisdom, the best hope for doing less harm in the world. Like punitive justice, it is painful in the extreme, but in the long run can yield precedents for a real remedy for barbarism.

UNESCO's Bad

March 12, 2012

Poor UNESCO, the UN's most underfunded agency. Well aware of the U.S. law forbidding U.S. contributions to an organization recognizing a Palestinian state, they went in anyway like a male praying mantis in heat, and "admitted" Palestine on Halloween 2011. Presto, a 22 percent reduction in an already strangled budget.

Now in an action March 8 in Paris, the Board voted 33 to 19 to take up Teodoro Obiang Nguema's offer of three million dollars for an award in his name – or actually, the "UNESCO-Equatorial Guinea Prize," for "quality of human life." The world press ridicules the act, and the outspoken Committee to Protect Journalists issued a statement the same day: "The 33 states who voted in favor have chosen to promote the image of President Obiang rather than uphold basic standards of human rights. They should be ashamed." An alert defender of the rights of journalists worldwide, CPJ knows whereof it speaks.

According to another UN body, the United Nations Development Programme, Equatorial Guinea was the worst country in the world in UNDP's 2011 Human Development Report, a reflection of available wealth compared to development. EG's per capita GDP—$19,000—would equal Hungary's or Poland's if it were equitably distributed, or twice that of Ecuador, Peru, or China. The problem is, over two-thirds of EG's unfortunate 700,000 souls get by on less than one dollar per day. Agence France Press, Associated Press, Human Rights Watch, and other agencies have had a field day pointing out these discrepancies.

The country was pretty bad under Obiang's predecessor and relative, Francisco Macias Nguema, who murdered one-quarter of the population until his own execution in 1979. The current president, who took over in a military coup the same year, got control of the country's oil reserves in the following 33 years, and amassed a good personal cushion of $600 million. His son's mansion at 3620 Sweetbriar Road, valued at $70 million, is the highest assessed property in Malibu, California. Another family property, at 42 Avenue Foch in Paris, comes in at $670 million if you count the Louis XV furniture and other appurtenances.

George Soros's Open Society Institute said earlier this year that, "Using UNESCO to try to assert legal prosecution from a criminal investigation just reinforces the sense that the Obiang family has no regard for the organization's mission – only how they can benefit from associating themselves with it."

South Africa's Desmond Tutu, also, was "deeply troubled by the well-documented record of human rights abuse, repression of press freedom and official corruption" in EG. He added in February, 2012, "The UNESCO-Obiang prize is irreversibly tainted by its association with the repression and high level of corruption of President Obiang's government."

EG employs a skillful Washington lobby group, Cassidy and Associates, at $120,000 per month (source: U.S. Justice Department) to burnish its image. In April of 2006, they snookered Secretary of State Condoleezza Rice into receiving Obiang warmly at a photo op, saying, "You are a good friend, and we welcome you." Her good friend's national radio had just broadcast that Obiang was in "permanent contact with the Almighty," and can "kill anyone without being called to account." Rice's handlers tried to distance her from Obiang after her gaffe, but the genie was out of the bottle. In 2006, we would take any friends who would have us.

Those of us who had checking accounts at Riggs Bank (1836-2005, R.I.P.) were not amused when the bank was brought down after investigations showed it was laundering Obiang's money. I kind of miss Riggs, its short name had an authoritative ring to it.

SecState Rice was not the only U.S. official to defend Obiang. While the 2008 State Department Human Rights report was pretty grisly—"a fully equipped torture room in the basement of the Bata Central Police Station… electric shocks with starter cables attached to different parts of the body with alligator clips; and various forms of suspension with hands and feet tied together for prolonged periods while security officials beat victims as they swung back and forth"—improvements were noted in the 2010 report: "Unlike the previous year, no journalists were arrested."

Al Kamen's *Washington Post* piece March 9 on this fiasco offers a ray of hope: "Despite UNESCO's inspired effort to discredit itself, the organization's legal office has determined that legal problems related to the name change and other matters may make it impossible to award the prize."

Tutu, still on the case, said, "Giving the prize a different name does nothing to answer these concerns or remove doubts about the origins of the funds that finance the award."

Yo, UNESCO, when in a ditch, stop digging.

I love UNESCO, its mission, its programs. I participated in one myself, last summer in Accra. It was an honor to the organization's real character. UNESCO's enlightened officials in Paris have also been stalwart supporters of media development in Africa and other regions.

But like virginity, credibility cannot be restored once it's lost. Time to sack the fools who took the organization into this rut, and return to its original mission. It is underfunded, but need not accept quarters for turning tricks.

A little spanking, then let's get on with it.

The Window That Went Around the World

March 14, 2012

Johannesburg was the established crime capital of South Africa in the hopeful 1990s. Later in the decade, the sleepier Pretoria made courageous inroads in crime statistics. This was never supposed to happen in South Africa's most "boring" city, which was considered by people in the Cape as "the largest cemetery in the world with traffic lights."

I liked Pretoria though, the tea gardens, the energizing climate, and the quick political and social changes visible in Nelson Mandela's marvelous creation. If you saw the movie *Invictus*, remember that the story started in Loftus Field, Pretoria's rugby stadium.

Every virtue has a corresponding vice, so in tranquil Pretoria, the newly invasive burglars violated not only many properties in every economic and social class, but also created dissonance with the grace of the city's jacaranda-lined streets.

After a couple of break-ins at my little row house on Arcadia Street (just two blocks from my office at the U.S. Embassy), I asked the security office for something called "dragons' teeth" – a line of jagged metal installed on the six-foot perimeter wall around the property, to discourage yet more intruders.

"It won't help," said the security man at the embassy. "The committed thief will just come over the wall with a mattress."

I was a little taken aback, but countered, "Maybe we could focus on the uncommitted thief? There must be plenty of those. Plus, I have never seen a thief in the street carrying a mattress, have you?"

"Fair enough," he said, and had the dragons' teeth installed. There were even a couple more break-and-enters after that in the property (thus proving the security official right), but not another into the house itself. Lawn furniture, outdoor lanterns, that sort of thing.

In March of 1997 I went to my right-hand drive Toyota parked in a back alley to take it to a work meeting, and found the passenger window smashed by burglars from the night before. There hadn't been much in the car to steal, and if they'd tried to hot-wire the car and make off with it, then they hadn't succeeded. So I was glad still to have a car, though a mutilated one.

It was easy enough to drive to the Toyota dealer two miles down the road. Toyota did a brisk business in Pretoria and the dealer had a state-of-the-art service section. I showed my problem to the technician, and he looked up the part in cut time in his catalogue.

"We don't carry that part," he said. "Not for the 1995 model."

(My car had come from the same shop, before I'd bought it second hand two years later.)

"Not carry the part?" I said. "But you sell the car here."

"We do. But the part isn't in my inventory. You'll have to order it from the U.S. or Japan or somewhere."

This discouraged me, but I called up a service called "Just Ask Janie," a clever business based at Dulles airport which located items of any sort which were unavailable in the various embassies, and also arranged for shipment and customs clearance. For an item as large as a car window (the item is twice the length of the window you actually see), the cost was pretty challenging.

After six weeks driving with tin foil in the passenger window, I was thrilled to receive the rather large box by air freight, with the part I needed to make the car whole again.

I opened the carton, and carefully slipped the large item out of its lengthy container.

The punch line: on the window itself, I peeled off a sticker saying, "Made in South Africa.

Mirabile dictu, the car part had been manufactured in South Africa for export only, had been shipped to the central Toyota headquarters in Japan, and from there to the U.S. for the American market. My window, shipped from IAD to JHB, had thereby circumnavigated the world, an instance of the marvels of globalization.

I am inspired when I think of the hardy item and its ability to make a full rotation around a 22,000 mile sphere and return to its place of origin.

Marvelous, what an interlocking world commercial system can achieve.

Grateful for the window, I felt better and made further forays into God's own earth in the far-flung regions of South Africa.

Mandela rallied people of all stripes to make an oddly connected system work for the general benefit. I honored him, and the intrepid Toyota dealership, and the courage of the single window that could.

Declinism in Decline

March 18, 2012

Some decades ago when SNL was still funny, they staged a panel discussion on "Women's Problems," staffed only by male chauvinists.

I'm not sure why this comes to mind, when hearing Americans discuss American decline. The notion has gotten a lot of attention since the economic debacle of 2008. Some of our periodicals devote entire issues to this single topic, and anyone who can get someone else's attention on the subject seems to make the best of it, pro or con or undecided. The more vivid depictions evoke unicorns and feathered serpents, and can make for energetic reading and listening. The first rendering of the unicorn, also, must have been a magical moment of human creative output, then must have tired after it became a branded reference and showed up in a lot of tapestries.

Declinism will be raised in the political debates of the coming months, in the same way that Jimmy Carter's adversaries effectively picked at his *fin de siècle* sighs and "malaise" statements of July 15, 1979. The speech actually never used the word "malaise," but

raised Carter's poll standings from around zero to 37 percent. In the longer run, it brought him down under the tsunami of Reagan optimism which had greater resonance with the American public. We may well see a restaging of this strategy later this year.

One of the rare credible voices in the current palaver is that of conservative commentator Robert Kagan, author of the recent book *The World America Made* (Knopf, 2012.). The book may lay the matter to rest, pointing out the indisputable: a world of unprecedented global prosperity even through recent vicissitudes of market spasms; sixty years without conflict among great powers; democracy in over 100 countries, compared to ten before World War II. In his incisive book, Kagan says, "Are Americans in danger of committing preemptive superpower suicide out of a misplaced fear of declining power?"

Case closed for the moment, until some candidate wants to flog a dead unicorn in the coming presidential campaign. Kagan says that any notion of past American omnipotence is chimerical, and that we never really had our way after all. Hence, no decline. This is powerful logic.

A Romney advisor, Kagan spoke March 15 at the American Enterprise Institute, delivering an off-the-cuff account of the notions in his book. NPR's Tom Gjelten artfully moderated the panel discussion, and joked about his own failure to spark controversy among experts from AEI, the New American Foundation, and Brookings. The panel found consensus that the declinism debate may finally have spun itself out. Elsewhere, Heritage says something similar. All claimed that the global structure currently owes its stability and flourishing to the United States, and that American decline would lead to a sort of new Dark Age of anarchy.

One awaits a European, Asian, African, or Latin American voice to verify or challenge these findings. None was present on March 15, unless you count Peter Bergen, the brilliant British-American who says "we" when referring to the United States.

Bolstered by others, Kagan's is a voice to be reckoned with. Listen for his ideas in future Romney articulations on the subject. What to do about Syrian massacres? "There will be no Syrian action before the election – maybe after." We will likely intervene after the U.S. elections, "If not, President Obama should not say, 'Assad must go.'"

Kagan's good joke March 15 was that his liberal friends had told him in 2008, "If I voted for McCain, we would invade yet another Muslim country. And they were right. I did vote for McCain, and we did."

One panelist ridiculed soft power as "squishy power, goofy power," and deserves some compassion for being on another planet during the past ten years. Much silliness is heard in the land about the irrelevance of the minds, hearts, and opinions of seven billion people. Kaiser Wilhelm, too, mistook arms and economy as the sole source of national strength. Such solipsisms have led mainly to war and defeat.

This was not part of Kagan's arguments, however. His hold up.

Competing think tanks now rise to a high level of civility and unanimity on the subject. March 15, all agreed with Kagan that if the

U.S. Congress savages the U.S. budget, we will lose hard power; that a consensus exists in the United States (and always did) that the United States should play a strong role in world affairs for its own, and the world's, interests. All agreed that the Ron Paul notion of retraction is a non-starter, and that the United States has a "special nature" (read: "exceptionalism").

None questioned that the rise of non-threatening powers such as India, Brazil, and others (China??) can be an advantage in a world where power and wealth are an expanding universe and not a zero sum game. Agreed: President Obama has intensified, not contracted, the combative stance of the United States in overseas conflicts.

Will the Chicago May NATO summit establish and finalize a SOFA (Status of Forces Agreement) with Afghanistan? Likely.

And the U.S. will certainly not seek to cut and run from Afghanistan in the near future, despite White House pronouncements to the contrary. Thus spake Bergen and others.

But the love feast was lacking a main course: might others see American declinism from other perspectives? Do alternative judgments exist of America's "unique" role in securing global peace? On this, we've had thin gruel, and could use some input on a matter that has been "settled" by American intellects. Friendly voices from outside might see us differently.

Lunch with Joe

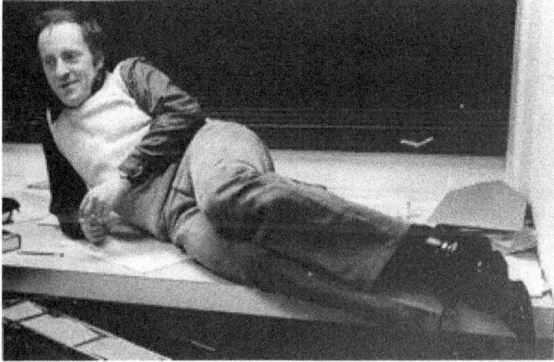

Terence A. Todman, one of the system's first African American ambassadors, was my first and best mentor. With Ambassador Todman, nothing was left to chance, and all organized events at his house had a purpose. He set high professional standards by precept and example, and noticed when Americans at a reception were losing valuable time by failing to mingle with guests of other nationalities.

In 1987 Joseph Brodsky landed the Nobel, and decided to come to Denmark to see about the sales of his works translated into Scandinavian languages. He believed poetry should be subsidized so more people could read it. Poetry collections should be left in lounges, airports, doctors' offices, instead of *Runner's World* and *Ingenue*.

The boss between Todman and me seized on the opportunity, and decided Danish contacts should be gathered around the ambassador's lunch table for the occasion.

"Let's get the Jewish community to meet him," she said. This sounded a little off to me.

"Do we know if he cares about being Jewish?" I asked. "Isn't poetry everything to him?"

"OK," she said. "Then invite some poets also." This mixture was certainly not the makeup of a coherent, Todmanesque session, but I understood the logistics were being "tasked" to me, and I was a junior officer under orders.

I'd been reading Brodsky's new essays, *Less Than One* (NY: Farrar, Strauss & Giroux, 1986). Its prose swept me away, as did the fanciful Leningrad he described in it. The motif of narrow waterways in the northern city of canals ("the Venice of the north") evoked a fairy land of gently urban elegance and beauty. Never mind that Brodsky's mother almost hadn't made it through the German "blockade" of the 1940s. Many had succumbed, but the city's serene beauty somehow prevailed. I even saw it myself in a weekend package trip there from my temporary home in Copenhagen.

I drew up a list of "invitees" which cleared muster almost without question, and the notices went out two weeks in advance in accordance with Danish custom. Danes loved Ambassador Todman. His Virgin Island background gave him a somewhat Danish identity even before they met him. More so when he quickly and adroitly caught on to their cultural quirks, and kidded them ever so gently about them.

Todman was an omnivorous reader, but hadn't taken on Brodsky, so I loaned him mine. This produced the first of several nasty rain clouds that formed over the event at his house.

Certain items in Brodsky's prose alarmed and offended the ambassador, and for good reason. I saw when I reread them myself. Brodsky's gorgeous prose included veiled references to dark-skinned people that were condescending and worse. He was Russian, after all. I had been too enthralled by the metaphors even to notice, the first time around.

As we sat together on the windy deck of a Baltic ferry, the ambassador said he was uncomfortable hosting such a writer, Nobel or not. I remembered my first moments of resistance to the whole idea for a lunch with no particular purpose, but couldn't naysay my immediate boss behind her back, it wasn't proper. So I took the hit.

I hoped the occasion might be saved by Brodsky's charm at lunch, but he wasn't charming at all. Visibly distressed by his own shortcomings with the English language, he lapsed into an impossible spaghetti of sentences of dependent clauses never seeming to start or finish. No one could make out what he was trying to say.

Todman, who always ran his lunches pedagogically, asked him some straight questions but got no straight answers. People stopped paying attention, and Brodsky trailed off into the void like a verbal robot, with looped and incomprehensible musings. He said he was fascinated by the Kattegat visible from the dining room window – the narrow stretch of water separating Denmark and Sweden just across the way.

Things degenerated. The guests became restless and unruly, and started roaming around the room. One asked another across the table for a light for his cigarette. To Todman's consternation and mine, the second one stood up and walked around to indulge his colleague, interrupting any possible train of thought.

At the least opportune moment, a young Danish poet stood up and recited some of her own work. This interested no one, but then neither did Brodsky, who kept getting lost in dependent English clauses and phrases he couldn't work his way out of.

Just for the occasion, a Russian émigré, fresh off the train from the Finland station himself, had bought a suit. Volodya had never before been to any embassy in any country, and was plenty nervous to be in this daunting setting. A brilliant journalist, he'd written a thesis on *Hamlet* and was learning Danish, but had never before been out of his country.

The general pandemonium annoyed the ambassador a lot. He was as if a commanding officer in an engagement not going according to plan, and had every reason to find revenge against those who had advised him so badly. No one else at the lunch seemed to care (except me).

One Danish journalist violated the universal rule of fork-in-hand-equals-off-the-record, and the next day published a comment Brodsky made to a dismayed Todman, "Mr. Ambassador, I have been to the residence of your colleague in Stockholm, and I can assure you that any Russian toilet has a more complete collection of world literature than your colleague had in his library." The chain reaction of irritants only intensified.

A climax was needed, something like a *Commedia dell'Arte* crashing of broken dishes off stage. The Filipino cook provided even better, emerging from the kitchen with an immense tray of dessert—very hot apple cobbler—and somehow splattered its top layer onto the back of the brand new suit jacket of the already intimidated Russian journalist, Volodya. In an unlikely maneuver even Charlie Chaplin might not have pulled off, the cook, trying to correct his faux pas, caught the serving tray in its fall. Instead of saving the situation, though, he ended up grinding the remains of the apple cobbler into the unfortunate Volodya's back, every gram of the scalding mass. This really happened. Volodya's back was burning but he was too frightened to move.

Brodsky saw this happen, but did not react, only kept yakking about some deficiencies of the world publishing system, and its moral obligation to subsidize poetry and get it into the hands of more people. The mediocre Danish poet stood up again and did another recitation. No one paid any attention at all.

The consummate diplomat, Ambassador Todman intoned just barely above the cacophony and instructed the guilty cook to take Volodya's jacket and get it to the dry cleaner ASAP.

Furious but magnanimous, the great Todman put an end to the debacle and got everyone out of his house. He never complained or punished anyone, though god knows he had reason to do so.

Looking for an application to the story? Volodya and I became life-long friends, and assist each other to this day.

In addition, the creators of the most sublime narratives sometimes lose their gloss in conversation, I think because it is painful to them to allow out a sentence or phrase less elegant than the polished ones they have labored over so intensely. The soaring heights of their achievements are realized in solitude, and can no more show through in spontaneity on demand, than a dancing monkey can conjugate Danish verbs or swim the length of the Kattegat against its idiosyncratic currents.

[Note: a couple of years later when Brodsky was named American poet laureate, I wrote to him from Spain and invited him to visit. He wrote back, "As you know, I have a fascination for narrow bodies of water. If you could include the Straits of Gibraltar in my visit, I will come." Schedules happen, and it never worked out. He died in 1996.]

Our Next Bubble

March 20, 2012

The difference between mortgages and student debt is that an education cannot be repossessed. Hence, we don't know how the next bubble will burst or what it will look like when it does, we know only that it is coming.

Over ninety percent of American undergraduates take on debt, and over 40 percent default. By 2013, student debt will exceed one trillion dollars nationwide, compared to $730 billion for auto loans and $693 billion in credit card debt.

The cruelty of this next economic debacle is in its needlessness, and in the self damage it will inflict on our beleaguered so-called system.

We know the basics already: $24,000 average debt on graduation with a B.A. degree, with restructuring mechanisms basically nil, and a relentless inflation not only of grades but of expectations by employers that their applicants come stuffed with degrees. Why? Because they can, there are so many graduates now around.

Not forever and not for much longer, say the analysts. The remains of the middle class are getting restive, and soon just won't be able to pony up. The pitchforks are gathering in the warehouses, in the form of educative abstinence and boycott. Even bankruptcy gives no relief to the debtor; our favorite lending institutions have fixed the system so that payback obligations march on even after bankruptcy filings. The fortress of the lenders has become impregnable against all battering rams.

"But it's expensive, and yields a fine product," say the system's defenders.

Yes, and yet. *The Economist*, not the most Jacobin of publications, says that a $45,000-a-year education can easily be reduced by two-thirds, just by having a look at middle management on our campuses.

The three books published in 2011 on this subject (see Benjamin Ginsberg, *The Fall of the Faculty*, Oxford University Press, 2011) draw the same conclusion, and further: mid level management not only sucks the oxygen out of academe, but also brings ludicrous cost increases to an overburdened consumer. Somehow from Socrates to Larry Summers, education happened without these shackling parasites. Their profession never even much existed until 20 years ago. After the earthquake in Haiti in January of 2010, a small group of Haitian undergrads approached an East Coast university, and asked their registrar for a three-week grace period on their January (spring) tuition. The school told them to pay or leave. They further degraded the students by offering them psychological counseling in lieu of a payment restructure, as if their troubles had been self-inflicted.

In March of 2012, a foreign student on the same campus saw an increase in tuition costs in mid-semester, contrary to a signed agreement between his funding source and the school charging the bills. When he asked for a short extension to meet the unexpected increase, he was told he should pay within four days or risk the loss of his student visa, and immediate deportation.

This ignominious behavior will only send students elsewhere to viable alternatives in Australia, UK, Canada, and South Africa. The creditors will conduct studies to find the cause of enrollment decreases, but anyone with eyes and ears could give them the conclusions from intuition, gratis.

It will be a pleasure to see the more wasteful and hardnosed institutions go under, and yet no one will benefit when they do so.

Never mind the debt: the *cost* of tertiary education in the United States is beyond sustainable levels. Universities are supposed to be smart, and should know what's coming. The disgrace, shame, and folly of it will suck in the perpetrators and the victims alike.

People can't and won't pay these bills forever, and the ancien régime will melt into the woodwork and retool themselves, when the regime collapses in, oh, about two years – unless a few of our 4,000 institutions of higher learning figure out how to reduce needless mid-level management and tuition to a sane level. Those who do will inherit the earth and the others will go where they deserve. Especially when it turns out people didn't need them after all.

Notes: As of 2005, administrators at 756,500 OUTNUMBERED 675,000 faculty. Since 1978, the cost of higher education has increased by 900 percent, 650 points above inflation. Administrative staffers on campuses have increased 240 percent. In the ten years between 2000 and 2010, the cost of college education at public institutions rose 37 percent, private institutions 25 percent. (Source: National Center for Education Statistics, 2006.)

This Week in Africa, Good News and Bad

March 27, 2012

For democratic succession, Senegal had a good day Sunday as bitter-ender Abdoulaye Wade conceded election defeat, then even called his former protégé Macky Sall, here pictured, to congratulate him on his 65-35 percent win. Long after he had outstayed his welcome, Wade was determined to plug along until the ballot boxes said otherwise. Not all countries are so fortunate.

By contrast, last week in Mali next door, a handful of lieutenants and captains seized power from elected President Amadou Toumani Touré, going into the last month of his term of office. Putschists under U.S.-trained Captain Amadou Sanogo cited inefficacy of President Touré's struggle against separatist Tuaregs in the north, mingled with al-Qaeda operatives and recently unemployed ex-mercenaries for Ghaddafi.

Faction within faction, some bad behavior resulted as rank and file soldiers got drunk and sacked the presidential palace like conquering Goths. Their leaders apologized, but were unable to say whether the ousted president was alive or dead.

March 24, enlightened crowds in Bamako created something called the United Front for the Safeguarding of Democracy and the Republic (FDR by its French acronym). In an impassioned written statement, the FDR called for return to democracy and the restoration of the Malian Constitution of 1991, which had defined putsches or coups as "an indefensible felony against the Malian people."

The news here is the tone and rhetoric of the manifesto. Evoking an earlier episode of revolutionary fervor from another continent, the document channels the spirit and format of the French Revolution. This, despite West Africa's grisly memories of French colonization, where French officials used to punish villagers who failed to pony up tribute and taxes for the occupiers. I once met an elderly Malian who said that as a child he had witnessed a head cracking between two boards of wood, attached at one end like a nutcracker.

The March 24 Manifesto is lengthy, but reads in part as follows:

> Whereas no Malian, nor any group of Malians, of whatever power, may suspend with a stroke of the pen a constitution adopted by referendum by the sovereign people of Mali...
>
> Whereas whatever act taken by the power of the State under the guise of exception seeking the submission of the citizens, whether by constitutional act or by communiqué, is strictly denied legality or legitimacy...

This lofty prose is remarkable in an age of sound bites and brevity. One imagines impassioned French Enlightenment activists mouthing the words. A glimpse of Jacques-Louis David's *Oath of the Tennis Court* recalls the adrenaline and fervor of the June 20, 1789 event staged on the site of the Jeu de Paume, once a royal tennis court and now a museum of impressionism at the Place de la Concorde in France's capital.

Love-hate for the French is pungent in France's former empire. After two centuries and some bitter memories, the previous colonies still make their appeals to a higher authority – not to a Deistic god nor to Allah, but in the manner of French Revolution rhetoric, to an

inanimate Rule of Law. The FDR manifesto reads like an incanta-
tion, including eleven "Whereas's" and exhorts citizens to act according to their higher nature – "We invite the international community to realize that Mali is traversing one of the darkest periods
of its history."

In pre-earthquake days in Haiti, Jean-Bertrand Aristide's supporters cried *"Aristide ou la Mort!"* on their rampages – a good mimicry
of *"La Liberté ou la Mort!"* from an earlier age. Words which thrill
even as they deceive.

Whether Tom Paine loaned the phrase to the French or vice versa,
its power crossed continents and oceans a century before telegra-
phy existed.

Likewise, Mali spurned De Gaulle's offer to be part of the franc
zone in 1960. Caught up in the later fervor of "Les Indépendences,"
Mali and Guinea both rejected offers they considered patronizing,
and invented new currencies for their independent countries – the
Malian franc and the Guinean franc, neither of which floated on
any European currency. To Guineans and Malians at the time, it
signified a clean break with their subservience under colonial rule.

The parallel between the March 24 Bamako manifesto and French
revolutionary rhetoric is unmistakable. Distressed and disenfran-
chised Malians appealed to the highest power imaginable (Reason,)
by evoking French proclamations of liberty in texts that bear the cadences of prayer. Rule of law, the intellect, a previous constitution
long since forgotten, and the derring-do of the Third Estate rising in
one voice at the Jeu de Paume – somehow the model remains, even
to those far removed in time and place from the original.

The rhetoric lives on in far-flung lands, carried by some almost untraceable intellectual DNA, appealing to a French model perform-
ing at its best. The process is at the same time a sterile chase after
chimera and myth, and an effective capture of an aesthetic which
rallied a nation (even in its moments of betrayal) over two centuries
ago. The original spirit may now be gone, but it lives in its yearn-

ings and the path of its trenchant logic. Here love and hate make a perfect union. The silly white wigs of Kenyan judges capture none of the intensity of these most ambivalent sentiments of France's universal appeal.

Cosmogony in a Coffee Tin

April 5, 2012

The Rosebud Lakota reservation in South Dakota had been closed to foreign visitors after a few murders nearby in Pine Ridge, in 1973. Six years later, the Academy for Educational Development got clearance to take a few and try it out. I went with six African visitors to see alternative education systems there. Though they spoke French, the six all had different mother tongues. This detail would be the revolver on the mantelpiece in a Chekhov play.

We stayed in rudimentary housing. Despite some charm to the serene landscape, the reservation was an open sore and a reminder of the calamities endured by the Lakota a century earlier. Nothing much happened during our ten-day visit. We saw an empty school, recently built by the federal government, but found no students, teachers or others during the weekday tour.

The one distraction in the area was a small food store with two aisles of dry goods. I drove the group there, and we made a thorough examination of the store's offerings.

A young man approached us in the flour and rice section of the store, and asked if we were the group from Africa. Pretty evidently, we were. He said he'd been sent to invite the visitors to a healing ceremony. I quickly polled the group and we all sought any distraction.

The young man gave me directions to a house at the top of a bluff, and asked us to return the following evening at seven. There weren't many landmarks in the terrain, so the route was clear. No blind alleys in the Lakota area of South Dakota.

When we arrived at dusk the following day, the young man greeted us at the door of the simple prairie structure. He guided us inside to a living area, and seated us in a circle on the dirt floor.

An ancient Lakota sage came out from a sleeping area and sat opposite us, speaking softly to the young man. We worked out the following and segued directly to the ceremony: the older man, mainly blind and marked by a scorched face and an expression of uncomplaining grief and weariness, would explain the procedure in his native Lakota, then the younger man would repeat in English for me to render into French for the guests.

Empty coffee tins lay at the four extremities of the room, representing the axes of the universe and its creation. In the space between, we were asked to imagine the infinite dimension of the Creation.

With solemnity and emotion, the older man recounted the Lakota version of the creation myth to present times. Tears first trickled, then flowed freely down his cheeks. After half an hour going through the story, the man returned from a sort of trance, and addressed the group directly, asking (in Lakota) who in the group had a close friend or family member in need of healing.

The Togolese school principal said his sister was ill back in Togo, and needed some assistance. So, guided by the elder, we focused attention on the distant Togolese woman.

We sensed relief after the emotional intensity of the ceremony. The coffee tins—the elder's only prop—became ordinary objects again, after having gained the status of the four compass points of the world. As we had all given into the mood of the ceremony, we became more of a social entity and began to converse. Then came the kicker: still speaking through the younger man's interpretation and mine, the elder said to the six Africans: "I have now given a healing ceremony with my best energies. I ask for only one thing in return." It seemed a reasonable request.

"I would like to know how my name sounds in your native tongues. I should explain that at the moment of my birth, it was prophesied that I would carry burning coals in my hands three times in my life, each time without affecting or burning the skin. The burning coal would be associated with my ability to heal, but my third use of this gift would coincide with my death. I have now had this opportunity twice, and I understand that one more remains, which I eagerly await, though I know I will die as it occurs."

The visitors listened closer.

"I ask, then, how you might express this notion in your native tongue, that is, 'He-who-carries-hot-coals-three-times-in-his-life-without-being-burned-and-is-to-die-the-third-time-he-employs-the-power.'"

There was silence in the room, and the six Africans became yet more contemplative.

"Do I ask for too much?" The elder pursued.

"No," said the Togolese, and rendered the phrase in his native Ewe in three short syllables, indicating to us all that the notion was a given—a commonplace, even—in his birthplace. A pretty complex notion for the questioning modernist, but an item of familiarity to others.

We went around the room, and each of the six using six unrelated languages, could also express the concept in two to three syllables. The vastness of such a coincidence settled in. No one had expected it, not even the elder.

We thanked the older man, then the younger, stayed awhile and then returned to the van outside and back to our dorm rooms, down the road.

There was nothing much to say about this unexpected finding. Inevitabilities of culture? Something about the wiring of the human brain? The logic of preindustrial and untrammeled consciousness? We never discussed it again. But the story remains, and is now told for anyone seeking to assign a meaning to it.

Inuits, Whales, Bach

April 24, 2012

The late Ingmar Egede was chancellor or headmaster, Teacher Trainers' School, Nuuk (the capital of Greenland.) As giant Greenland is a protectorate of tiny Denmark, it was included in my "area of operations" when I was press officer in Copenhagen and writing speeches there for U.S. Ambassador Terence Todman.

In 1988 when a class of 50 was to graduate in Nuuk, Ingmar called me in Copenhagen and said, "Bring your viola to the graduation, we will play Greenlandic folk songs for the ceremony." I did, and we did. It was a brilliant and even warm June afternoon.

The audience was meant to sing along, but not many had heard a string ensemble before, and the simple music stood alone in a stupor of general fascination. The graduating girls wore gorgeous apparel with beaded garments, the boys trundled in with jeans and T-shirts.

Six months later the graduating class went on its traditional celebratory trip – previously to Moscow and Tokyo, but I suggested

Washington, so they went there. Ingmar was suspicious of U.S. capitalism and predatory American practices, but willing to subject his students to these in a one-week trip to Washington and New York. Greenland's largest "city" has a population of 5,000. When the Teachers' Training School class took the New York subway for the first time, one of them said, "The airplane was an hallucination, New York was a fantasy, the subway was a confused dream."

Ingmar and I walked down the streets of New York, then Philadelphia, talking about things. He told me about his experiences with whales from the northern sectors of his country – he would embark in his motorized boat, and the whales would follow out of curiosity, spouting and playing in the grey waters off the coast, seeming to seek to communicate with him.

During World War II he had been taken from Thule, in Greenland's northern extremities, and planted in Denmark for his high school and college training. There had been concern that the Nazis would try to take Greenland, in their quest to dominate the North Atlantic. Ingmar's Danish became fluent during his years in Copenhagen, but he lost his native Inuit until relearning it from scratch after the end of the War. A transplant in 1946, he relearned the survival techniques of northern Greenlanders, and their maddeningly difficult dialect when it came time to reintegrate himself into his remote, northern habitat.

Like most Greenlanders, he was a racial composite, derived from the Inuits who previously inhabited his country, and the Danes who came later to colonize and mate with the locals. Regaining his native Greenlandic in his twenties, he straddled the European and the native elements of his peculiar culture. He was a leader in the Inuit Circumpolar Conference (ICC), which matched oral traditions for original inhabitants of the far north of Canada, Russia, Scandinavia, and Greenland, to trace migrations of peoples in the far north.

When his students passed by Yankee Stadium with me in a bus, to the bravado of the driver saying "90,000 capacity!" one of them said, "That is more than the entire population of our country." (The real capacity of Yankee Stadium is 52,000, but New York bus drivers love their stats.)

Ingmar and I walked down a street in Greenwich Village on a cold November evening of the same year, and heard a street musician cranking out a convincing version of a Bach sonata for solo flute. We had just been talking about the mysteries of communication with whales in the northernmost waters of the globe.

I said, "Reminds me of a violinist I heard on West Eighth Street years ago, playing the Bach Chaconne…" and then I stopped, realizing the irrelevance of my conversation. Ingmar said, "Yes, the d minor. I used to play it." That would be from his Copenhagen years, before he returned to the far north in the late 40s to hunt walrus and share moments with whales off the coast.

So. It is everywhere, the loftiest of European achievements. If in Greenland, then everywhere. Ingmar and I stepped into a tavern and followed our conversation's whimsy. I admired Bach, and Ingmar, and myself. Universals happen, one shouldn't be taken by surprise by mankind's achievements and the cherishing of its remarkable outputs.

With his passing, the d minor Chaconne will be taken up by another, and another, as the love for it extends far beyond the country of its origin. It always has, and will, until global warming puts an end to it.

Malamud and Me

April 27, 2012

Now after 32 years, I present to you my correspondence with Bernard Malamud, March 15 and April 14, 1981.

As the only American in the English department at Marien Ngouabi University (Brazzaville, Congo), I was tagged in December 1980 when a Congolese member of the department skipped the country to take a Fulbright in the U.S. He'd made his students sit for the exam on *The Assistant* by Bernard Malamud, then disappeared— poof—without a trace. Students roamed around the courtyard of the campus like lost herds, asking what to do and where to go.

The Language Department chairman asked me to grade the exams the students had written for the professor on the lam. I said Sure. I got a copy of Malamud's *The Assistant* around Christmas time, and tried to up my expertise in a writer and subject I knew little about. Such revelations, in the essays written at that time: the People's Republic of the Congo was a Marxist regime. Getting ahead meant

learning the language of social Darwinism and the evils of capitalism. The students had learned well from the Congolese professor,
and found innovative ways to despise the American system.
One student wrote the following:

> All and sundry consider righteously Frank Alpine as the
> main character in Bernard Malamud's book, "The Assis-
> tant." In his novel, Malamud, in keeping with the sacred
> rules of the novel WHICH ARE BOTH MYTH, FICTION
> AND REALITY, HAD DEPICTED Frank Alpine as one as
> much Praiseworthy as Blameworthy; indeed his whole
> lifetime was a terrible successions of ups and downs so far
> as he had committed devlish and holy deeds. This, he was
> said: "both good and evil character."
> Frank Alpine is but five and twenty, he spent a little
> part of his childhood in Orphan-house. From Italian origin,
> the young boy has to face alone the struggle for survival,
> whereas, country where he is living is ruled by the Jungle
> Law. Moreover, He is not a WASP (white anglo-saxon Prot-
> estant) therefore he is a victim of religious and racial ani-
> mosity...Frank Alpine is in some extent the embodiment of
> struggle led by the oppressed people in USA, the most pow-
> erful capitalistic nation, which is as an animal organism, in
> which money flows like blood in vein.
> Frank Alpine's Personality suscites many a turmoil
> among readers, who do not hesitate to criticize it bitterly. He
> is frivolous, naïve, burglar, mischievous, therefore a devil-
> ish character, and with a horrid, horrible personality....His
> personality symbolized the irony of fate. At the end of the
> book he converts into Jewish religion, he gets circumcised
> and become a full-fledged Jew, this a example of cowardice,
> of lack of confidence in himself, of lack of personality...He
> planned to be Jew just to get spiritual tranquility, but not
> vital elements for Life, he is very naïve. Unless we are intel-
> lectually one-eyed, or else, we can only approve and disap-
> prove the two-ness of FRANK Alpine's Personality.
> We conclude by saying that through his simplified style,
> Bernard MALAMUD presents to us One Frank Alpine, such

as is any young poor man in USA, not to choose good and let bad, but to extract beyond his painting the substance of his message in a trivial literature. [Big *sic* on all the above.]

In the days before photocopiers and even mimeo machines were available in Central Africa, I typed out the exam and sent it by mail to a friend of the scheduler in Malamud's medical office in New York. Malamud responded by return mail April 14, 1981:

> This is the year of *The Assistant* as examination material. It is being used by the French in this year's *aggregation*, and now here's your letter with news from the Congo.
>
> I think the best statement I've read on my work—eloquent and unarguable—begins "All and sundry righteously consider Frank Alpine as the main character in Bernard Malamud's book *The Assistant*."
>
> Otherwise the statement is not bad because it moves in the direction of the truth.
>
> Thank you very much for informing me.
>
> (Signed, Bernard Malamud)

Pace Paul Malamud, Bernard's son whom I valued as a colleague in the U.S. Information Agency in the 1980s and '90s.

The Sinologist in Each of Us

May 4, 2012

Now that a blind human rights activist is being seriously hassled in Dongshigu Village and/or Beijing, everyone is a Sinologist. I am not minimizing his plight, or the distemper of a nasty regime prepping itself to take over the world.

Only last month we were all experts on a place called Sanford, Florida, but in a rapidly shrinking public attention deficit, topics drawing our attention have the life spans of mayflies.

It is almost too easy to say,"They should pay attention to more things," and by the way, op/eds from many sources say so every day. I only wonder what form of shame could bring our impoverished media to order, and get them to tell us something other than anecdotes.

Poor Chen Guancheng makes great copy. He got into hot water by denouncing a government for imposing abortions in a one-child policy. He's blind. He escaped house detention, and managed as an individual to sidetrack the most important summit of the month. I am not claiming any malice on his part! My question is, did anything else happen in the world in the past week?

Even the best news corporations cut their overseas bureaus and rely on underpaid and clueless stringers. They say there is no market for the type of news they would like to be able to afford, but this hypothesis has not been put to the test. Something like the economic austerity gang, they cut the trunk of the tree to make the limbs grow. I am not a gardener but I think this does not favor the trees.

February 25-28, 2008, food riots broke out in a half dozen countries as the price of rice soared. Those who took to the streets got almost no attention in the world's media, I think because the stringers never took down their names, and lacked the talent to see anecdotes in the story. Twenty or 150 were killed in Cameroon by orders of President Paul Biya, depending on whose version you believe.

April 17, 2012, three weeks ago, Biya's former Prime Minister Inoni Ephraim (2004-2009) was hauled off to jail under the harsh lights of local television, weeping like an infant. Somehow the national airline, Camair, had gone broke under his watch, and someone had to be blamed.

North American investors came to meet Inoni in 2005, 2006, and 2007, to offer $100 million and fix Camair while safeguarding its name and personnel. They asked only that the books be revealed to them, not for purposes of prosecution, but as a way of fixing its dysfunction. The new Camair would have established daily nonstop flights from Atlanta to Douala, the main port in Central Africa, within two weeks. Even the corrupt would have benefited immeasurably, but lord forbid, others would have benefited as well. The Balkan says, "Make me blind in one eye" when told by the genie in the bottle that he could have anything he desired, but that his rivals would get the same blessing twice over. Like this, Cameroonian officials deep-ditched the deal and ruined it for everyone.

I don't know the exact role of Inoni in this sordid affair, but he was the obstacle to a system which would have given a spurt to a flagging economy in a region of tens of millions of entrepreneurial citizens now suffering to purchase rice for their families.

Sounds like a rant on Cameroon, right? Truly I take this as a case study only. Did the *New York Times* cover this significant story affecting tens of millions? Or any network or cable news service? It's a mere example of the shameful deficit of information we get, from those with the means and smarts and fancy university diplomas to do better. There are tons more.

I once witnessed a "debate" in Cleveland, between the editor of the *Plain Dealer* there, and Carl Stokes, who had once been mayor and went off in 1972 to New York to be a glitzy news anchor at WNBC-NY. The subject for discussion was the deficiencies of world news coverage in the U.S. media. Both sides of the "debate" were in full agreement that the job was being done superbly. When a gentleman in a turban stood up in the audience and said, "I am from India, which is a pretty big country, but I've seen no reference to my country in the U.S. media in the past year," Stokes said (this is a quote,) "Oh, if it's specialized news of that sort you are looking for, you should seek out the *Village Voice*."

China used to be the place in the world which was the farthest from home, except maybe for Sri Lanka, which we used to call Ceylon. But now we're all experts. We (Americans) are provincial, and well meaning, it's our charm and always will be. But if we mean to survive in a global world we largely created, we need a government economic stimulus now, and a little more awareness of what goes on outside our borders and coasts. This won't be fixed any time soon, but squeal we must in the meantime, like stuck pigs, underserved by the lazy-bones who presume to inform us.

At the Feet of the Master

May 7, 2012

Ten of us had Vernon Walters to ourselves, in a location in Scandinavia. Even he never predicted exactly what would happen later that year, but in 1989 he brought us fresh news of subtle changes affecting East-West relations. He'd been sent as President Reagan's ambassador to something called the Federal Republic of Germany, which no longer exists.

He was bewilderingly smart. He'd never been to college. He spoke perfect French, Spanish, Portuguese, Italian, Russian, and passable German. Everyone who ever met him had a Walters story. He was "General," or "Ambassador," depending on where he was at the time.

Talking as always without notes, he gave us updates and also reminded us of things we already half knew. Too smart for optimism, he sketched a working plan for straightening out the edges and angles of a fizzling conflict. He never said it would be settled soon. He was of the Ramrod School, figuring how to face the Soviet Union down at its own game.

Sometimes during a 90-minute brief, the listener wants to consider response, question, reflection, assimilation. None of that was called for with Walters: even the political counselor in the room settled back with a primary school receptivity. Dispute and refinement were pointless.

I don't know if he could have pulled it off without his amiable jowls, which followed his racing jaw like clouds retreating from an invisible wind.

He was funny, encyclopedic, avuncular, just as the legend which preceded him. Twenty years earlier, he'd been told off by a Soviet diplomat in Brazil that Americans lack the "Slavic ear" for languages. He'd responded in perfect Russian, "Perhaps your Excellency would prefer that we speak in Portuguese?"

The Soviet had growled in return, "Sir, you are a capable military professional, but no diplomat."

One day such stories will be told about those presently in the field, but they haven't emerged yet.

Listening to Walters was like a feast which never fattens. He was chunky himself, and played his role as if from Central Casting, only Central Casting could never have conveyed the lines so spontaneously. Peter Sellers, George C. Scott were brilliant, but could never have played him, and it's a good thing they never tried.

The best one-liner of the Cold War came out at the briefing – or the greatest I've heard. I often wondered since, if it was something Walters ever labored over or acquired from another. No matter, the delivery was the point.

"I was talking with my Soviet colleague in Bonn last week, and I told him, 'You see the problem here: in our system we have a fixed past and a moveable future. In yours, it's the opposite.'"

One cannot imagine the Soviet Ambassador's reaction, except maybe as a moment of rage or exhilaration. I still wonder that the line never gained the currency it deserved.

Seven months later, the Berlin Wall came down.

Sony Lab'ou Tansi (1947-1995)

May 8, 2012

He was born Marcel Ntsoni in Kimwaanza, of the then Belgian Congo. He was schooled mainly on the other side of the River, where the flag slogan still reads, "He who touches me will be free," addressed to subjects of King Leopold's larger, more hellish Congo. I took him and three others to a retreat in northern New Hampshire in the summer of 1978 (that's another story.) He disappeared into his room for four days and came out with a wide grin and the completed manuscript of *La Vie et demie,* published a year later by Les Éditions du Seuil. He never mentioned it, but he gave me a little wink in the novel by naming of one the streets "la rue Whitman."

For his novels and plays of rage and spite, he won the Grand Prix Littéraire d'Afrique in 1983, and the Palme de la Francophonie in 1985. Hachette and Seuil were his publishers.

He was enamored of Alfred Jarry (who in his situation wouldn't be!) and directed *Ubu Roi* in Brazzaville's Rocado Zulu Theatre, which he created. I was present one humid evening in 1980, and remember thinking, "*Macbeth* next, the ultimate text to counter tyrants." Sony was intrigued by the idea but never got around to staging it.

In the Fall of 1979 I had moved into a two-room, no-water flat in Brazzaville's university housing, and set up to teach English for a year. Sony and I were pretty busy that year, but we met a few times in the breezy city which had become a place of literary ferment when the Free French chose it as their capital in exile, during World War II.

One afternoon someone got hold of a Renault 4L, and four of us drove to the city's outskirts with Sony at the wheel. At a small bridge over a narrow waterway, a nervous soldier demanded our papers. Imprudently we had all gone out without any, except Sony himself. He winked to me in the back seat, then handed the same picture ID four separate times to the baffled soldier. The soldier waved us on, and Sony's wink turned to a wide grin. This taught me about his pluck and my own timid scruples.

At a conference two years later in France, a debate considered the ethics and aesthetics of African authors publishing in European languages (Sony's vernacular was Kikongo). He brought the house down that day with ridicule for those who defended the vernacular for sentimental reasons. How could his rage, ideas, innovations have escaped an archipelago of dusty villages, and reached an international audience – in a language other than French?

"The French school was straightforward," he argued. "The penalty for speaking local languages was to wear a cord around our necks, with a wood box filled with shit. When we tired of walking around with shit hanging from our necks, we took French as our language, end of story." You needn't love the oppressor to follow rules that made sense.

The People's Republic of the Congo decided to hold legitimate elections in 1992. President Sassou Nguesso hadn't advanced the country much. But he'd opted for the only large power willing to take it on, in their case the USSR.

When the chance of a real election came up, Sony partnered with opposition leader Bernard Kouléla, who had just been released after ten years as political prisoner. With two others, they traveled to Washington to seek backing for the campaign. With persistence and unlikely coincidence, they found me in very temporary digs. The five of us met for a drink on a hot summer night in Washington's West End.

"We need support from the international community," they said to me expectantly.

I asked what the agenda was of their new party, the MCDDI (Congolese Movement for Democracy and Integral Development). They said, "What's an agenda?" They were high spirited and prepared to take on the leadership of their country.

"You know," I said. "Like socialist? Or conservative, or progressive, or the party of fiscal restraint?"

"We need to know why you ask," Kouléla countered.

"Well there's the Socialist International for that program, or the Liberal International for the other. Are you left or right, would you say?"

This stumped them. Sony said, "We never discussed it. Our only platform is for the full flourishing of the human being." How could I not side with them?

They lost the national election, but Kouléla got the mayoral post for the capital, and Sony became the parliamentary delegate from Makélékélé, a section of Brazzaville.

The winner of the 1992 election, former PM Pascal Lissouba, was not amused. He devised minor punishments to the opposition, including pulling their passports. Sony might have used his to get some treatment for his HIV turned to AIDS.

He never got to leave again. I would still be looking even now for support for the MCDDI, but for the breakup of an inspired social movement. They might have ruled Congo with old-fashioned straight talk and transparency. AIDS took Sony in 1995.

In 1998 the little Congo broke out into unprecedented mayhem, with ethnic groups in the city fighting and exterminating each other. The Americans evacuated across the river to Kinshasa, to get out of the crossfire.

Sony was long gone by then. I still see him in his Jacobin hat, his grace and acceptance of everyone he ever met, and his nerve, countering corruption and tyranny wherever it popped up, with the potent arms of disgust and ridicule.

Lowering the Volume

May 9, 2012

If there were an example of the one percent, it would be someone who made $19,740,023 in 2010 – $1,930,000 of it in salary, the rest in benefits. These were the earnings of Jim McNerney, Chairman, President and CEO of Boeing. The point here is not to begrudge him of it.

He was interviewed May 9 by *Financial Times* U.S. Chief Commentator Ed Luce, before an audience at Washington's National Airport, at a public showing of Boeing's new "Dreamliner" – comparable in size to previous jumbo jets, but with 20 percent less fuel intake, and new technology to reduce drag and noise. The noise is said to be reduced by 60 percent over similarly sized aircraft, and the CO_2 emissions down by 20 percent.

In a U.S. economy which recorded a trade deficit of $46 billion for the single month of February, 2012, the aerospace industry in the U.S. recorded the largest net exports of any industry. The Aerospace Industries Association (AIA) recorded $220 billion in sales (domestic and international) for 2011. Ninety billion came in the form of trade surplus in the aerospace sector from overseas sales.

238

This is pretty big stuff, and merits a close listen.

McNerney makes no bones about who he is or what he seeks. He wants wealth restored to the United States, and wants a share of it for himself. Appointed as Chairman of President Obama's Export Council, he talks to the White House on a regular basis. He tells them what his industry needs from government, they tell him they will see about reconciling conflicting political voices, many of the latter sounding off from both sides at high decibels.
After the debt crisis debacle of summer, 2011, McNerney wrote the following (*Wall Street Journal*, October 31, 2011):

> For the good of the nation, our elected leaders must now find it within themselves to pass sound laws, regulate judiciously, and put aside escalating tactical political battles. If the super committee succeeds [it did not], the White House and congress should build on the moment and: Enact comprehensive, pro-growth tax reform that benefits everyone; Proceed with regulatory reform; and Reform and restructure existing entitlement programs.

Volatile stuff, and yet does this not call for serious attention and discussion??

May 9, Luce and McNerney spoke about the $18 billion investment by Boeing which yielded the 787 Dreamliner, and which now has orders from a half dozen countries, including Japan, UAE, and others.

In an echo chamber we would all like to escape, the shouters are reciting shorter and more repetitive catechisms. In fact sequestration (the just punishment for the failure of the super committee last summer) is killing all of us, and McNerney states this up front as the one bogey man surely we can all fear and loathe together. This is the start of the dialogue we need.

The stimulus that Nobel Prize winners Joseph Stieglitz and Paul Krugman call for so convincingly never came up in the conversation May 9. McNerney might be an agnostic or a believer in this axiomatic remedy, but it's not his job to opine. With decency and dignity, he didn't. Could it be that the one strongest factor in reversing America's trade deficit – aerospace – might actually find peace with the viable prophets calling for the Keynesian solutions we might all take as givens at this point?

The circus barkers tossing around austerity like exhausted whiffle balls might silence themselves long enough to listen to the pros. I don't know if Krugman, Stieglitz and McNerney have ever been in a room together, but I imagine those three could get us out of this hideous mess if we could get them together. The surgeon is not the anesthesiologist and vice versa, but put them in the room and let each do the job, and the outcome just might work.

When the Boeing 707 was put on the market in the 1960s, the United States pulled 50 per cent of the world's economy. Now it is half that. No huge problem there, as we still do pretty well for five percent of the world's population. McNerney did comment on this, and showed low stress levels. Take what's given, and proceed. The U.S. is likely to make it through the current downturn, he said to Luce – with the fact that the country has done so seven times since its creation not as "proof," but as a sign of a likely way forward.

240

Before 9/11, aerospace R and D was fixated on speed. Now with fuel prices rising, says McNerney, efficiency and load capacity are the only rational goals to have. "The Chinese will get to that," he argues, so let's get on with it ourselves.

Aerospace 3.5 million Americans in every state of the country. Time to listen attentively to those who have figured out how to do this. "Ultimately we are pragmatic people. We are not Fox and CNN," McNerney said affably at the end of his talk. Luce countered, "Surely you meant MSNBC?"

"Please Go Away"

May 15, 2012

That was the slogan on the marquee of Boston's Crimson Travel Agency, for about two decades.

Early in 1973 I took them up on it. Almost resolutely I entered the office and asked for the next plane to Africa. I was well aware of the Continent's immensity, but I felt I needed to depart quickly, so I asked where I could go without a visa.

"If you consider Morocco as part of Africa," they said, "then Casablanca. Thursday night."

My sense of urgency was not only compulsion, but pent-up demand and release from half a decade as draft bait.

Once in Morocco I was able to get a visa for Senegal, and from there, another for Mali, and so forth. I don't remember how flexible the itinerary was, but somehow I made it from one destination to the next with an old-fashioned paper ticket.

In Ouagadougou an African friend sent the houseboy to the airport to "pick me up" in the very early morning. And so he did, on a bicycle, which carried my luggage while the servant and I walked. It was still dark.

I dozed on a plastic chaise-longue on my host's patio awaiting dawn. When the sun rose, I saw dozens of vultures starting their day from a nearby roof. I asked the young man with the bicycle if these were indeed vultures (Ouagadougou's trash removal network).

He corrected me: *"Non Monsieur. Ça, c'est des pigeons."*

In Bamako I was stunned by the March heat, and managed only to lift a finger every half hour to ask for more juice or tonic. I took a plane to Timbuktu and saw a serene village with ancient overtones, never again to exist now that al-Qaeda in the Maghreb (AQIM) has taken over the area.

The trip was a birth of sorts. No traveler to Africa forgets the first impression on seeing the Continent. In my case, it was from an airplane window on the landing approach, exchanging glances with a shepherd below in a blue robe, from 200 feet above. The glance lasted only a couple of seconds because of the speed of the landing plane. The shepherd seemed to say to me, "From whence do you come, and for what purpose?

When I returned to Boston after a month away, I saw my arithmetic blunder which had made it all possible: I had embarked thinking that I had two thousand dollars in my account – one thousand for the trip, a thousand more as financial cushion for when I returned.

In fact I had never "borrowed" in a pretty simple column of numbers, and with the miscalculation now corrected, I saw that what remained was not really a thousand, but in fact zero.

This was not a good feeling, but I made it to the taxi dispatch office and survived for a year on cab receipts shared 50/50 with the company.

But for my bad arithmetic, I would never have made it to the birth-place of humanity and the next phase of the discoveries I needed to make on my own.